DATE NIGHT IDEAS FOR COUPLES

DATE NIGHT IDEAS
FOR COUPLES

Fun Ways to Connect with Your Partner for an Entertaining Night

ANGELA NICOLE HOLTON

ROCKRIDGE
PRESS

First Rockridge Press trade paperback edition 2023

Rockridge Press and the Rockridge Press logo are trademarks or registered trademarks of Callisto Media Inc. and/or its affiliates in the United States and other countries and may not be used without written permission.

For general information on our other products and services, please contact our Customer Care Department within the United States at (866) 744-2665, or outside the United States at (510) 253-0500.

Paperback ISBN: 979-8-88650-827-7 | eBook ISBN: 979-8-88650-831-4

Manufactured in the United States of America

Interior and Cover Designer: Jake Flaherty
Art Producer: Samantha Ulban
Editor: Kahlil Thomas
Production Editor: Emily Sheehan
Production Manager: David Zapanta

Illustrations by Shutterstock: © Olha Saiuk: xii; © a1. DESIGN: 17; © Zoran Milic: 18; © m2art: 33; © etraveler: 34; © sodesignby: 48; © Bonna Shejve: 63; © Vector Tradition: 78; © mapush: 91; © morokey: 92; © liu_miu: 105; © Tribalium: 106
© Collaborate Agency: xi, 64
Author photo courtesy of Regan Rouse Photography

10 9 8 7 6 5 4 3 2 1 0

For Nana, our cherished Matriarch and GRANDmother. Thank you for this blessing, our first brainchild. I love and miss you eternally.

CONTENTS

Introduction

Welcome to your exclusive couples' date-night resource book. If this book has found its way into your hands, congratulations! You've taken the first step toward gaining greater control of your dating relationship and creating love that's more intentional. Great relationships don't just happen automatically. They require steady intention, attention, and deliberate action.

My name is Angela Nicole Holton, and I'm a dating and relationship coach, creator of the Conscious Love and Dating Method, and author of *The Secret Method to Conscious Love*. My work has been shared with thousands of individuals around the world and has helped them create richer, happier, and healthier dating and love relationships. I love witnessing happy couples, and one of my goals in service to our world is to support more people in finding and maintaining healthy love relationships.

A relationship is a like a living organism: If it is not nurtured, it cannot thrive and eventually it dies off without consistent time and attention. Regular dates are the key to sustaining a viable and loving relationship, particularly for long-term relationships or marriages, when couples begin to settle into security and comfort, and sometimes grow complacent.

Embracing dating in a relationship keeps it fresh, passionate, and enjoyable. Dating in relationships is important for creating quality time together, strengthening bonds, building unity and greater self-expression, deepening communication, creating new memories, eliminating boredom, expressing affection, and prioritizing one another.

This book helps you avoid the frustration that sometimes comes from lacking original date ideas. Here, the legwork is done for you! You will find dates that involve art and creativity, sensuality and sexuality, romance, cooking and dining, playful competition, adventure, spontaneity, nostalgia, group activities, and fantasy and play. According to psychoanalyst Dr. Laurie Hollman, play and fantasy are important for adults, who mostly function in logic, for enhancing creativity, emotional regulation, and mood. Better moods mean better connection and more fun with our partners. So, in addition to growing closer to your partner, be prepared to have lots of fun!

Whether you want to surprise your partner with dates or plan them together, these recommendations will help spark deeper curiosity, communication, playfulness, passion, understanding, and emotional and physical intimacy for an overall better relationship.

How to Use This Book

The dates within this book are separated into eight different chapters that each offer alternatives to your typical clichéd date nights. Each date includes a brief description of the date; a road map to help you plan and put the date into action; samples of suggested conversation starters to spark more meaningful dialogue and communication and opportunities to learn more about your partner; and, finally, a level-up section to help you expand on the date with greater elaboration and sometimes greater financial costs.

That said, the dates are designed with all budgets in mind. Many of them require only your time, energy, and imagination. It's up to you how detailed and elaborate you'd like your dates to be.

You can also choose your preference in how you interact with the book. Whether you read and follow the dates from start to finish, flip through the book and choose dates randomly, or choose specific ideas based on your ability, mood, and time considerations, you get to create your own dating adventures! Some of the dates are seasonal, but modifications are suggested to suit all climates.

Let the dating begin!

"Tying the Knot," page 9

Paint the Landscape of Your Lives, page 6

CHAPTER 1

Instead of Netflix and Chill . . .

L et's face it: "Netflix and chill," though an easy and inexpensive date, is not the most imaginative rendezvous and might not score points with your partner. This is especially true if their love language—the way they receive love—is "quality time." Even if you're on a college budget, a Netflix and chill evening isn't necessarily the best approach to building deeper intimacy and connection in your relationship.

"Intimacy" is described as closeness between people in a relationship. It is not necessarily synonymous with "sex," which is often connoted in a date like this. It's possible to have sex without intimacy as well as intimacy without sex. There are different types of intimacy that can grow in romantic relationships, including emotional, physical, intellectual, spiritual, and experiential (sharing common interests and activities). According to a 2019 *Healthline* article, these different types of intimacy are based on seven key factors: honesty, trust, safety, communication, affection, compassion, and acceptance. This section includes dates that will support you in building intimacy by expanding date ideas beyond the typical movie night at home, bringing more spice, laughter, and interaction to your time together.

NAME THAT MOVIE LINE

This home activity takes movie watching up a notch by bringing games, creativity, and connection into your living room.

MAKE A PLAN

- This date won't cost you anything! It requires only a blindfold and access to YouTube. This game is played until there's a winner.
- Blindfold your partner and play them a clip of a line from a classic or favorite film. Give your partner 60 seconds to guess the movie title. Then it's your turn.
- The first person to reach 10 points chooses the next date-night movie.

START A CONVERSATION

- What are your top five favorite movies and characters, and why?
- What is your favorite movie genre and decade?
- Which movies did you watch as a child with your family?
- If you could be any movie superhero, who would you be and why?
- Who is your favorite actor and why?

LEVEL UP

Take this date outside of your living room and explore a day of spontaneous movie hopping. Have each partner randomly select a movie, perhaps with a little background on the movie's synopsis, to watch at a movie theater. Discuss them afterward. If it's summertime, search for a free movie night at a local park and take a picnic for two. To satisfy your intellectual curiosity, find a lecture discussion on one of the latest movies.

THE "PEACE" TO YOUR PUZZLE

During this activity you'll put pieces of a puzzle together. This will promote peace and relaxation, and at the same time stimulate your brains and your partnership through joint effort.

MAKE A PLAN

- Prior to your date, select a 300-piece puzzle to assemble. You can find puzzles at bookstores, toy stores, or thrift shops. The goal is to complete the puzzle in one evening. Choose a puzzle with a theme that resonates with you, whether it's cars, travel, food, animals, or architecture.
- Find a cozy and comfortable place to assemble the puzzle.
- Prepare snacks and drinks to enjoy when you're piecing together the puzzle.
- Play calming or romantic music to enhance the ambiance.
- Don't stop until the puzzle is complete. You can make it more challenging by setting a timeline for completion.

START A CONVERSATION

- I wish I had learned to . . .
- When I can't figure things out on my own I . . .
- One activity that relieves stress and anxiety for me is . . .
- My strengths are . . .
- My weaknesses are . . .

LEVEL UP

Connecting with a partner doesn't always have to rely on physical or emotional intimacy. Intellectual intimacy is also key to getting closer in a relationship. Level up this date by trying a more complex puzzle with 500 or 1,000 pieces—which may require a series of dates. You may also invite another couple to join you one evening for dinner and a puzzle.

COUPLE'S YOGA AT HOME

Move over, Twister—tonight's date is a sensual couple's yoga experience at home. This activity allows you to explore trust and passion in your relationship.

MAKE A PLAN

- For tonight's date you will need a couple's yoga video class to follow, two yoga mats or blankets, and comfortable, stretchy clothes. Some classes require pillows and straps, so have those handy, too.

- Download or livestream a couple's yoga class or YouTube tutorial.

- Set up a comfortable yoga space in your home using candles, incense, and essential oils. You can also incorporate a meditation together before starting the class to help you relax.

- Try adding some "pleasure talk," such as, "How does this feel?" or, "Does it feel good when we do this?"

START A CONVERSATION

- Did you enjoy yoga together? What feelings came up for you?

- Would you want to do this again? Would you consider taking an in-person class together?

- Describe your experience of intimacy with one another during the class. Did you feel more connected? Trusting and safe? Openly vulnerable? Self-conscious?

LEVEL UP

Level up this date by practicing nude yoga together at home or register for a traditional, in-person couples' yoga class. Notice the difference and preference of doing couple's yoga in person or at home. Afterward, share what you liked and disliked. What thoughts and feelings came up for each of you? Were you able to relax? Were you self-conscious or embarrassed?

PAINT THE LANDSCAPE OF YOUR LIVES

Time to get imaginative and paint a masterpiece together.

MAKE A PLAN

- This activity requires a painting canvas or a piece of paper that you and your partner will build on together. You'll also need acrylic or oil paints, watercolors, markers, or colored pencils, and paintbrushes, if using.
- You can find affordable supplies at a local craft store or dollar shop.
- Play classical music to enhance your creative expression.
- Take turns painting or drawing for five minutes at a time. Use a timer to steer each partner away from "perfecting" the picture during their turn.
- Let go of any judgment. Just have fun.

START A CONVERSATION

- Notice during the activity if either of you experienced judgment or shame about your own work. Did you feel bored, scared, self-conscious, or nervous?
- Tell your partner about your favorite artists and styles, and why. Do you like abstract art? Realism? Impressionism? Van Gogh, Picasso, or Basquiat? Consider exploring new artists together.

LEVEL UP

Build on your creativity by taking an art class together or exploring local museums and art galleries. Many museums operate by donation, so you may fancy an afternoon of museum hopping. You can also take a sip-and-paint class or hire a local artist for a Sunday brunch or couples' night. To keep it even simpler, you can purchase adult coloring books and paint-by-number activities for future dates together.

TRUTH OR DARE?

This teenage throwback game comes with a warning label. Be sure you are prepared to listen and answer all truths—and tackle any daring dares.

MAKE A PLAN

- This date won't require much—just a pen, a dozen or more slips of paper, and a jar, plus some snacks to enjoy while you play.

- Decide in advance if certain questions are off limits and then fill out each slip of paper with a question to answer truthfully or a dare to complete. Fold the paper in half and place it in the jar.

- Pull a paper from the jar and either answer the question or complete the dare.

- All acts must happen safely inside of the home and can't be put off for another day.

START A CONVERSATION

- How much trust do we have in our relationship?

- How can we deepen our trust in the relationship?

- What's the biggest "white lie" you've ever told?

- If you could tell a lie that would benefit you and your loved ones, and you knew for certain you wouldn't get caught, would you do it?

- If it feels safe, you can ask each other, "What's your biggest secret?"

To take this date even deeper, experiment with trust exercises. You can try an exercise called the "eye gaze." Sit facing one another with your hearts leveled. Gently gaze into one another's eyes. Set a timer for one minute and do your best not to take your gaze off your partner. Notice how you feel. Talk to your partner about what came up for both of you.

"TYING THE KNOT"

Remember sack races in school, where you and a partner would each place one leg inside a sack and race to the finish line? Today, you will use a string to tie yourselves together, relying on mutual dependence to accomplish a goal.

MAKE A PLAN

- All you'll need are two long pieces of string or rope and an activity to accomplish together.

- Tie yourselves together, tying one string around your inner legs or ankles and the other string around your inner arms or wrists.

- Choose an activity to accomplish together, such as preparing dinner, washing the dishes, or cleaning the yard.

- For the next hour you will be "joined at the hip" as you work together to complete the task. You cannot separate or use any body parts that are tied together.

START A CONVERSATION

- Which hobby or activity could you join in together that requires both of your concerted efforts to achieve a goal?

- Are there areas in the relationship where you desire more help from your partner?

- When is it hard for you to ask for help?

LEVEL UP

If you want to take this date deeper, try a couples' *Amazing Race*-style challenge where you compete with other couples to achieve an adventurous goal, like a DIY obstacle course or a hiking or climbing course. Although you each may have your own individual hobbies, and independence is vital for a healthy relationship, finding a joined, common interest that relies on interdependence can strengthen your connection, security, safety, and communication.

MAKE BEAUTIFUL MUSIC TOGETHER

Tonight, make your love a melody by creating your own relationship playlist. Include your cherished love songs as a couple, as well as individual favorites.

MAKE A PLAN

- All you'll need for this date is a smart device, a music streaming platform, and a few hours of uninterrupted quality time.

- Have each partner choose songs to add to your "lovers' playlist." Add songs that will make you think of your partner when they're not with you.

- Jam out together to your new music compilation or enjoy a quiet night of romance with your new sounds.

START A CONVERSATION

- What are your favorite songs and musical genres? What did you grow up listening to?

- If you have different preferences in music, talk about your differences and ways you can compromise so that each partner's musical preference feels supported.

- Educate one another on your different music styles. What is most meaningful to you about your favorite music?

- What song makes you think of your partner?

LEVEL UP

No matter what your tastes are, finding music compatibility can bring you even closer together. For your next date, scout some local live music events or concerts. Find a free music event or plan your next date night at a bar or lounge with deejay music or a classic jukebox. If you both have an appreciation for music, consider taking deejaying or music lessons together.

OH YEAH—IT'S '80S NIGHT

Whether or not you grew up in the '80s, who doesn't love the music, movies, and fashion of this colorful decade? Throw it back to this wacky era and dress the part, coupled with a movie from the decade.

MAKE A PLAN

- When it comes to fashion, bright colors, fabrics, patterns, and mix-and-match describe this decade (think Madonna, Prince, or Boy George). Reach into your drawers or scour thrift stores for cheap and fun outfits inspired by '80s fashion.

- Make your movie selections. Maybe you love teen classics like *The Breakfast Club*, action hits like *Top Gun*, or rom-coms like *When Harry Met Sally*. Pick at least one that appeals to each of you.

START A CONVERSATION

- How many '80s movies do you know? How many have you seen? See how many '80s movies you and your partner can come up with together and write them down.

- Music in the '80s, from R&B to pop, was also quite memorable. Call out as many songs as you and your partner can bring to mind. Bonus points if you can remember the music video.

LEVEL UP

Arcades, fast food, and endless walking around shopping malls, hand locked with your sweetheart's, were popular teen dates in the '80s. Take this date a step further and choose an '80s-themed date outside of your home. You might get lucky and find a shopping mall, fast food, and an arcade all in one.

LET'S BUILD A FORT TOGETHER

During this activity, you'll create some nostalgia together as you build a fort in the comfort of your own home. This date captures the innocence and fun of childhood.

MAKE A PLAN

- This activity is perfect for a Friday or Saturday evening or a weekend morning.
- Gather blankets, pillows, flashlights, rope or string, chairs, flameless candles, tables, sticks (broom, mop), blocks, and any other creative supplies to build your fort.
- Be imaginative and make your fort intricate, maybe including tunnels and hideaways.
- Grab some treats to eat inside your fort with flameless, battery-powered candles.
- Bring a couple of board games inside for extra nostalgia, or get cozy and let romance take its course.

START A CONVERSATION

- What's your favorite childhood memory?
- What did you want to be when you grew up?
- What were you afraid of as a child?
- What was your favorite candy as a child?
- Who was your favorite teacher?
- What got you into trouble as a kid?

Take your fort adventure outdoors and plan a weekend camping or "glamping" trip to a state park or camping site. You can make s'mores and bring your favorite childhood snacks, games, and music. If you're not a camper, take a drive to a beautiful nature spot and book a log cabin or a room at a charming, rustic, and inexpensive bed and breakfast.

DIY "HOT" FUDGE SUNDAES

Bring the ice cream and all the fixin's. You and your partner are having a night of childhood nostalgia mixed with adult sensuality and pleasure.

MAKE A PLAN

- For this DIY activity, you will need to shop in advance for all your favorite sundae ingredients. Be as creative as you want!

- Challenge each other to see who can build the largest sundae.

- Swap sundaes, feed your partner their sundae, and then swap passionate kisses . . . only!

- Enjoy your sensual evening without other distractions.

START A CONVERSATION

- Do you share intimate kisses as often as you prefer?

- Do you still enjoy kissing one another? How can you improve your kissing?

- What is your favorite body part to kiss? To be kissed?

- Can you spend more time kissing that doesn't always lead to sex?

- Where is your favorite place to kiss?

- What do you think is the best movie kissing/sex scene of all time?

LEVEL UP

Take this sensual date further and explore books and movies on eroticism that might improve or deepen your sexual connection. If you've been together a long time and sex and intimacy have waned, consider taking a sex class together, visiting a sex and pleasure shop, or working with a sex therapist. If you enjoyed the playful aspect of this date, on your next date take your dessert (and a kiss) to a park or on a daytime or evening stroll.

SATURDAY MORNING NAUGHTINESS . . . TOGETHER?

Intimacy and sex can become less spontaneous in long-term relationships. Sometimes life gets in the way, with children, work, family, and other responsibilities. This date allows spontaneous and adventurous intimacy with your partner but makes sure you set aside time for physical intimacy. So ditch the weekend chores and create some Saturday morning fun with reenactments of your favorite steamy romantic movie scenes.

MAKE A PLAN

- Before the date, have each partner select their movie, grab any necessary props, and set up the scene.
- Movie ideas might include *Dirty Dancing*, *Pretty Woman*, *9½ Weeks*, *Like Water for Chocolate*, *Titanic*, *Love Jones*, *The Notebook*, *Call Me by Your Name*, *Ghost*, *Carol*, *An Officer and a Gentleman*, or *Fifty Shades of Grey*.
- You can watch the movie and "act" along or make it up as you go.
- Try letting go of inhibitions and any embarrassment with your partner and just be yourself. Give yourself permission to *have fun*!

START A CONVERSATION

- Are you enjoying this date? If not, what would you enjoy more?
- What are some of your likes and dislikes in the bedroom?
- What was your favorite part of the reenactment?
- Do you spend enough time connecting through sexual intimacy? If not, how can you create more time and space for connection?
- Do you ever feel awkward and uncomfortable or that you can't fully be yourself with your partner?
- What excites you in life? What frightens you?

- How were emotions and affection expressed in your family growing up?

This was already a risqué and adventurous date, but you can take it one step further by repeating this date as a preplanned or spontaneous surprise to your partner, perhaps trying a different movie. Role-playing is also another way to bring greater intimacy into a relationship. Choose your favorite movie characters and play their roles during dinner and "dessert." Or attend a masquerade or erotic-themed party. Netflix and chill has its proper time and place, but it won't always be a great way to connect with your partner. This activity is a great way to carve out meaningful time with your partner.

Make Beautiful Music Together, page 10

Pins, Balls, and Darts, page 27

CHAPTER 2

Instead of Dinner and a Movie . . .

I t's Friday night and you hear the familiar words from your partner, "Do you want to go to dinner and a movie tonight?" You feign excitement, but deep down you're thinking, "Again?"

The "dinner and a movie" date is like "old wine in a new bottle." Even my late 98-year-old grandmother used to go to "the picture show and dinner." This popular date allows time for bonding and romance over dinner, but although the movie element may encompass *some* PDA, it prevents couples from engaging *more* deeply in talking, sharing, and touching. And this once-popular date night may be beginning to see its end, with higher ticket prices, lower attendance since the COVID-19 pandemic, and more streaming movies available at home. Couples are now exploring cheaper options for movie dates.

Whether you're wanting to blossom a new relationship or reignite the spark and intimacy in a long-term commitment, exploring more innovative ways to spend time together might be the antidote you're searching for. Instead of dinner and a movie, this chapter explores unique and more exciting ways to connect with your partner that bring a mix of fun, creativity, pleasure, and adventure. Some of them won't cost a thing, and others are still less than the cost of dinner and a movie.

YOUR LOVE CONSTELLATION

Tonight your romance is filled with twinkles and sparkles as you plan an evening of stargazing.

MAKE A PLAN

- Check the weather in advance and choose an evening when the skies will be relatively clear and the winds will be low. For an even better experience, download a stargazing app.
- If you live in a big city with skyscrapers, you may want to drive to a more remote area like the beach, mountains, countryside, or a park that's away from the lights and noise.
- Pack a romantic picnic dinner with a blanket and candles and a lighter (or flameless candles).
- Be sure to spend moments in total silence gazing at the stars. It's a powerful experience!

CONVERSATIONS STARTERS

- Do you believe there is life on other planets?
- How do you think all the planets and galaxies came to be?
- If you could experience life on another planet, which one would you choose?
- If you went in to space and could only take five items, what would you bring?

LEVEL UP

In a newer relationship we often talk more to cover seemingly awkward moments, but as our relationship grows, silence becomes more natural and comfortable. Although leaning too heavily into silence can indicate other challenges, sharing moments of silence is an important part of a healthy relationship. If you're in a newer dating relationship, take this date to the next level by planning some quiet time at home together.

A DRIVE WITH RADIO ROULETTE

An old-fashioned teenage pastime is brought back tonight as you and your love take a drive and play a game of radio roulette.

MAKE A PLAN

- All you'll need for this activity is a car with a radio, or satellite radio, and your smartphone.
- Download the popular music discovery app Shazam.
- Turn the car radio on and set it to "scan."
- With each new station, try to be the first to guess the artist before the radio skips to the next station. Whoever is the first to guess correctly wins a point. If you're unsure of the artist or if both of you can't agree, use the Shazam app to verify the artist.
- The first person to 10 points wins and chooses dinner that night.

START A CONVERSATION

- What's your favorite family pastime?
- If you could go back and live in a different era, which one would it be?
- If you could have dinner with five musical artists, living or dead, whom would you choose?
- If you were stranded on an island and could only listen to the same five albums, which ones would you want?

LEVEL UP

Make this date even more special by planning a longer road or day trip. During the drive, listen to the playlist that you and your partner created in chapter 1 (page 10). If it suits the budget, rent a convertible or a classic vintage car for a day and go for a romantic drive or a day trip.

DATE NIGHT IN THE PARK

Take your typical dinner-and-movie night to the park and experience a night of romance and connection under the beautiful dark skies.

MAKE A PLAN

- Plan ahead and check the weather.
- Find a movie night in a local park or bring a movie on your own device.
- Pack a romantic dinner picnic (blanket, flameless or actual candles, dinner, drinks, and dessert).

START A CONVERSATION

- What was popular when you were a kid that you wish was still around?
- What is the best part about doing things outdoors?
- If you could star in your own television show or movie, what would it be about?
- If someone was playing you in a movie, who would it be?
- Who is your biggest celebrity crush?

LEVEL UP

You can level up this classic date by going on a mindful walk through the park together and discussing your different observations. Take one another to your favorite parts of the park and explain why you love them.

FANCY SOME BALLROOM DANCING?

It's time for you to take your moves to the ballroom and enjoy a fun (or clumsy!) night of ballroom dancing. Let's tangoooo!

MAKE A PLAN

- Each partner can research the different styles of ballroom dance in advance and decide which one they'd most like to learn. Swing, waltz, tango, mambo—there are so many to choose from.
- Sign up for a dance class at a local school, register for an online master class, or watch a YouTube tutorial.
- Choose your outfit—you'll want to look nice but be comfortable, with light, breathable fabrics. And don't forget your dancing shoes!

START A CONVERSATION

- Did you feel trusted or able to trust when you were dancing?
- Before this activity, how open were you to trying ballroom dancing? Was there one in particular you always wanted to learn?
- Do you prefer being a leader or follower in a group?
- Were you embarrassed, and how do you cope with moments of awkwardness?
- When have you laughed the most at yourself?
- What was the most embarrassing moment in your life?

LEVEL UP

Sign up for regular classes at a studio together. Don't worry, you won't be the only beginners! You may find that regular lessons offer exercise, relieve stress, enhance teamwork, and build trust. Consider going even further with this date by participating in an amateur dance contest. If you got the "jitter" bug, make a date of attending a dance performance contest and watch the pros, or curl up at home with some popcorn and watch *Dancing with the Stars*.

ROLLER BOOGIE NIGHTS

Ditch the car—you're riding on four wheels tonight. Revisit a favorite childhood activity and go to "boogie wonderland" on roller skates.

MAKE A PLAN

- Find a skating rink in your area, preferably one that hosts couples' night. Some cities offer outdoor skating. Check your local park or recreation guide.
- All you'll need is the price of admission and comfortable clothes.
- Most rinks include skate rentals, but check in advance about bringing your own.
- To recapture your youth, have dinner at the skating rink. Pizza, hot dogs, nachos, pretzels—oh yeah!
- Ask the deejay to play your favorite couples' song.

START A CONVERSATION

- What was your favorite childhood activity?
- What was/is your favorite dessert?
- What was your favorite childhood toy?
- If you had a time machine, which period of your life would you travel back to and why?
- If you could start over, having either all the money you need for the rest of your life or all the knowledge to get you through life successfully, which would you choose?

LEVEL UP

Plan a skating night with friends and other couples, or consider taking lessons or starting your own adult skating club. You can plan weekly or monthly dates to meet at a nearby park and hone your skills. Want to travel back in time? Schedule your next birthday party or big celebration at a roller-skating rink, or plan an easy but competitive roller derby with friends.

YOUR LAST FIRST DATE!

Surprise your partner with a reenactment of your first date together. Whether this is your tenth or hundredth date, tonight, you will reignite the spark that Cupid struck.

MAKE A PLAN

- For this special surprise date, recall as many details as you can of that first date and do your best to recreate them.
- If you still have (and can still fit in) the lucky outfit that sealed the deal with your lover, wear it.
- See how much you and your partner can recapture from that special date, such as sitting at the same table; ordering the same dishes, drinks, or desserts; and recounting the same conversation.

START A CONVERSATION

- Describe the worst date you've experienced.
- What do you like more about our relationship now than you did when we first met?
- How can we improve our relationship?
- What are five favorite things about our relationship?

LEVEL UP

Who says you have to wait until your annual anniversary to celebrate love? Isn't every day you've invested in your love and relationship cause for celebration? Level up this date by planning your next date as your special "anniversary" date. Pull out all the stops and revel in the magic of your relationship. Celebrate your commitment and devotion to one another, and the sacrifices and promises you've poured into the relationship so far. Love is worth celebrating!

PINS, BALLS, AND DARTS

Whether you were rebellious or studious as a teen, tonight you'll go back to your teenage years and hit the town for some bowling, pool, and video games.

MAKE A PLAN

- Ransack your closet for clothes from your youth and plan to visit a local multi-entertainment complex. No cover charge, but you'll need funds for the games.
- Some places charge by the hour for activities, some may require bowling lane reservations, and some may still use quarters for the arcade. Check ahead and come prepared.
- Select prizes together at the end of the night.
- Dinner is all the junk food you can eat, of course.
- Whoever wins one of your themed games chooses the next date night out.

START A CONVERSATION

- What was your greatest fear as a teenager?
- What sage advice would you go back and give your teenage self?
- What was the biggest trouble you ever got into as a teenager?
- Describe a time you may have succumbed to peer pressure as a teenager.

LEVEL UP

We've all likely seen romantic movies where two lovebirds visit a fair and kiss when they're riding the Ferris wheel, walk and hold hands, and share cotton candy. One lover wins a stuffed animal and presents it to the other. You get the idea. Take this date to the next level by reenacting this classic romantic portrayal. Find a town fair or festival and enjoy a night of teenage games, laughter, food, and sweets.

BURLESQUE YOUR HEARTS AWAY

Erotic sensuality, self-exploration, and entertainment collide for this thrilling and scintillating adventure with your partner. Tonight, you're surprising your lover at home with a private burlesque performance by you.

MAKE A PLAN

- Before your date, explore training videos to learn a short dance sequence and choose the music for your performance.

- Create an outfit that makes you feel sexy—from your closet, a thrift shop, or a costume rental.

- Tell your partner you have a surprise for them and cover their eyes with a blindfold. Then come out ready to turn your partner on and blow their mind.

START A CONVERSATION

- Did you enjoy performing for your partner? Did anything make you nervous, embarrassed, or uncomfortable?

- Ask your partner what they enjoyed most about your performance.

- If you had zero inhibitions and no fear of being judged or shamed, what sexual act or experience would you engage in?

- Discuss your ideas around sexual shame.

- If you had to choose one, would you be a voyeur or exhibitionist?

LEVEL UP

To level up this experience and explore hedonistic desires, attend a burlesque or striptease show together in person. If you're really feeling brave, join a couples' intimacy retreat or take a couples' sex class or workshop. Or try an erotic dance or pole dancing lesson to surprise your partner on a future date, or plan a short trip to the city of hedonistic desires: Las Vegas.

YOU'RE SCORING TONIGHT!

No, not like that. Tonight you will be spectators at a professional or amateur sporting event.

MAKE A PLAN

- Purchase tickets for one of your favorite team's games, whether it's football, basketball, baseball, hockey, soccer, or something else.
- If you don't want to break the bank, attend a local college or high school game.
- Outdoor nighttime events can be cold. Plan for the weather.

START A CONVERSATION

- What's your favorite sports team?
- Who is your all-time favorite athlete, living or dead?
- If you could be a professional sports player, which sport would you play?
- If you were a team mascot, what would you be?

LEVEL UP

Take this date up a notch by playing a sport instead of watching. Join a coed team game with other couples. Whether it's softball, golf, bowling, or tennis, playing sports together strengthens your relationship by building trust, increasing adrenaline, and promoting cooperation. Remember to keep it fun and light on the competition. After your game, grab some pizza at a local restaurant and let the bonding continue.

DINNER IN THE DARK

Immerse your senses in a unique dining experience as you and your partner enjoy a three-course dinner at home in total darkness.

MAKE A PLAN

- Plan a three-course meal at home. Bring in foods that have diverse and unique textures, temperatures, and smells and exotic flavors. Perhaps some dishes are eaten with fingers and hands, or chopsticks, or sipped directly from a bowl or straw.

- Blindfold your partner and notice their reactions as they taste, touch, smell, and feel each dish, and which senses become heightened.

- Have your partner describe their experience and guess the foods and flavors they are tasting by touch, taste, smell, and sound alone.

START A CONVERSATION

- What were your favorite foods as a kid?

- Which foods did you dislike as a kid that you now enjoy?

- Did you feel safety and trust during this exercise? Which foods felt or tasted unusual? Which were intimidating to taste/touch?

- If you could eat only one food for the rest of your life, what would it be?

- Do you prefer sweet, sour, spicy, salty, or tangy?

LEVEL UP

Research a dine-in-the-dark experience and level up your date. If you're ready to turn on some serious heat, dive even deeper into sensual immersion. Use everyday food items from your kitchen's pantry or refrigerator for a blind taste-and-touch test using condiments, spices, sweets, and sauces, but . . . no clothes! Blindfold your lover and drizzle different foods into their mouth and onto their body. Of course, you have to taste it as well!

BAE AND BOOKS

For this daytime activity, you and your partner are "hitting" both the bookstore and on each other. Today, you'll pretend you're meeting for the very first time.

MAKE A PLAN

- Visit a bookstore or library and as you're both perusing the books and magazines, role-play meeting for the very first time. Decide who initiates contact and then let it roll.

- Give each other a few minutes to browse before you start talking. Don't just pretend to shop; really browse with interest. Ask your partner questions about the books they're looking at. Make it a goal to find out something new about each other, like you're meeting for the first time.

- What looks good to you? Share and discuss the most interesting books and magazines you can find.

- For some nostalgic fun, head over to the children's section and read a children's story to each other.

START A CONVERSATION

- Did you like role-playing? Was it fun? Corny?
- Can you name a role-playing scene you fantasize about?
- How do you feel about adding role-playing to your relationship?
- What's the best pickup line you've ever heard?
- What's the worst pickup line you've ever heard?
- Who's your favorite author? Favorite book? Favorite book genre?
- In school, did you prefer math and science or reading and writing?
- What would be the title of your memoir or autobiography?

In a 2022 Marriage.com article, Rachael Pace explains intellectual intimacy as being comfortable sharing ideas and thoughts with each other, even if you disagree. Intellectual compatibility can increase your bond and make the relationship even more exciting as you learn about each other on a deeper level. Level up this date by expanding your intellectual intimacy and curiosity with an afternoon or evening of literature education. Attend a book seminar or a book signing event, or watch a virtual book signing. Follow your book event with an intimate "dine and discuss" date.

Roller Boogie Nights, page 25

CHAPTER 3

Instead of a Walk in the Park...

Taking a walk together in the park isn't a bad date idea. In fact, walking together as a couple is a wonderful way to decompress from the day's stress, limit distractions, engage in PDA, and introduce more thoughtful and intentional communication into your partnership, allowing time to address more challenging, "hot topic" conversations that may arouse sensitive emotions. Walking together, especially hand in hand, isn't just very intimate; it's very personal as well. Adding the element of nature can further reduce the stress and tension associated with our daily lives, not to mention the stress from any existing relationship problems.

But is this actually a date? Or part of your daily routine as a couple? What happens when the "date" is always a spur of the moment walk in the park and not a preplanned or surprise outing? Preplanned dates are important to implement in your relationship in order to create that special feeling of "date night" for each partner. According to popular counseling practice Couples Therapy Inc., "A *Date Night* definition includes a sense of leaving the ordinary realm of daily experience. You dress differently. You go to a different place or engage in an unusual activity that isn't part of your daily routine. *Date Nights* are unique, and out of the ordinary."

This section includes dates designed to help you and your partner experience more novelty in your dating life, and still create the time and space for meaningful conversations and special moments to connect. Some of the dates do include nature, but with an added twist. The dates are mostly designed as daytime activities; however, you can switch any of them up and make them evening dates.

VOLUNTEER FOR A CAUSE

Volunteering as a couple can strengthen your bond by supporting shared interests and values and connecting to your community. Choose a cause you both believe in.

MAKE A PLAN

- This date is a freebie in dollars, but an investment of your time and energy.
- Research organizations near you—an animal shelter, a park conservation group, a soup kitchen, a school, or a senior facility.
- Plan to designate a minimum of two hours to volunteer. Some places may have a set blocked time for volunteers.

START A CONVERSATION

- Where, if at all, have you volunteered in the past? What was the most rewarding part about it? What was the most challenging?
- Name five core values that are important to you.
- If you could solve just one of the world's problems, which one would you choose?
- If you could select this year's Nobel Peace Prize recipient, whom would you choose?
- If you could travel anywhere in the world to volunteer, where would you go and what would you do?
- Who is your greatest hero? Why?

LEVEL UP

To take this date to the next level, you and your partner can sign up for regular volunteer projects each month. You may choose a different cause each time, and invite family and friends to join you. To take it even further, plan your next vacation as a volunteer trip or designate a portion of your vacation for volunteerism.

SPEAKING YOUR LOVE LANGUAGES

Each partner will choose an activity that relates to their love language—the way each person needs to give and receive love—and help the other partner learn to speak it.

MAKE A PLAN

- First, read *The 5 Love Languages* by Gary Chapman to learn your love languages. If you're pressed for time, you can take the five-minute online quiz instead of reading the book. (The link to the quiz is in the Resources section on page 122.)

- Each partner can choose an activity for their part of the date. For instance, if receiving gifts is your love language, you could go shopping together for a small gift. If your language is acts of service, your partner can help you with a home-improvement project.

START A CONVERSATION

- Did your love language surprise you? Why or why not? Were you surprised by your partner's?

- How was your love language spoken to you as a child?

- What is your favorite type of PDA?

- What are five characteristics that best describe you?

- What words of affirmation brighten your smile? What do you like to hear most from your partner?

LEVEL UP

To take your date one step further, incorporate this date into your monthly dating routine. Designate time at least once per month to spend a day speaking your partner's love language consciously and intentionally. Together, write a list of different activities you can participate in that speak each other's love language, and pick one each month to share with your partner.

SIGHTS AND SELFIES

Take a tour of your city's historical sites and snap selfies to capture your adventures together. Let your photos tell a story on social media or create a photo album just for yourselves.

MAKE A PLAN

- Prior to your date, map out the historical sites you plan to visit. Be sure you have enough storage on your smartphones to photograph your outing, or bring a camera.
- Check ahead for reservations, admission fees, and hours of operation.
- Take selfies of the two of you together capturing the historical sites behind you, such as a monument, building or park.
- Try to visit at least two or three different sites.
- Post your selfies to social media or place them in an album.

START A CONVERSATION

- What do you think makes a good picture?
- What was your worst school picture taken?
- What is your favorite picture of yourself? Of your partner? Together?
- What kinds of historical sites do you like to visit most (if at all) and why?

LEVEL UP

There are so many fun ways to level up this date: Book a professional photo shoot for just the two of you (a nude or semi-nude shoot if you're feeling frisky); stage a coordinated color or fun themed photo shoot (western, medieval, Roaring '20s); save on money with a DIY photo shoot at home using your smartphone's photo timer; or take a photography class together.

A TRIP TO THE BOTANICAL GARDEN

Today's stroll is not your typical walk in the park. Enjoy smelling the roses with your partner as you plan a day to peruse a local botanical garden.

MAKE A PLAN

- Not much effort is required for this date. Plan to spend the afternoon here. You may need to purchase tickets in advance. You may also want to pack a good camera.

- Do some research to see if your town has a botanical garden. If you can't find a garden, spend an afternoon visiting different plant and floral nurseries in your area.

- Even in the winter months, many botanical gardens have beautiful indoor nurseries or other exhibits.

- Plan an afternoon to walk around the garden and choose your favorite flowers and plants.

START A CONVERSATION

- What is your favorite flower? Why?

- If you were a plant or flower, which would you be and why?

- What did you learn most about your partner from their flower choice? Were there new insights or surprises?

- What interests you most about the natural, physical world?

LEVEL UP

If this activity sparked a green thumb in either of you, you can take this date further by creating your own flower garden at home. If you don't have access to a yard, or if that sounds too daunting, start with planters. Still intimidated? Consider buying a plant that symbolizes your relationship, then name and nurture it together. You can also level up this date with a virtual or in-person floral design class. Check local offers or visit the New York Botanical Garden site (NYBG.org) for virtual design classes.

GO ON A LOVERS' HIKE

Grab your snacks and packs, and head for the trails. You're going for a hike today and basking in the splendor of nature.

MAKE A PLAN

- The remarkable aspect of Mother Nature is that she's everywhere we look. You'll need a few hours or less, depending on how long you'd like to hike. If you don't live near a hiking area, factor in driving time as well.

- Plan ahead for weather.

- Pull out your guidebooks and choose your hiking trail. Consider one you haven't experienced before. You can find beautiful and romantic trails on sites like AllTrails (AllTrails.com), and choose ones based on length, scenery, and level of difficulty.

- Pack snacks, hydration, bug spray, and outerwear.

START A CONVERSATION

- Do you prefer the beach or mountains? Ocean or lake? What is most meaningful to you about your choice?

- If you could visit any natural landmark in the world (Niagara Falls, the Grand Canyon, Mount Everest), what would it be and why?

- Have you ever encountered a wild animal in nature? What was it, and what did you do?

- What was your favorite place to visit when you were a kid?

LEVEL UP

To level up this date, you and your partner can join a hiking club. This will create time and space for you to regularly enjoy intimate and memorable moments together in nature, as well as allow you to meet new people. You can take this date even further by planning your next vacation around visiting a scenic hiking trail in another country, or search for others to add to your couple's bucket list.

THRIFT SHOPPIN' HOPPIN' TOGETHER

Whether it's classic vintage clothing or an antique steal for the home, who doesn't love a good bargain? Visit some thrift stores, antique shops, or flea markets and hunt for those treasures together.

MAKE A PLAN

- This activity, inspired by one of my favorite pastimes with an old boyfriend, requires a few hours for antiquing or hopping around thrift shops. Many cities have shopping districts or historical areas specifically dedicated to antique shopping.
- For more fun, set a goal, whether it's finding the best deal or discovering the weirdest or most unusual item.
- Agree on a budget ahead of time to alleviate financial disagreements, and discuss the rules of engagement, such as agreeing on purchases or not judging style.

START A CONVERSATION

- What is your favorite room in a house?
- What decorating style speaks to you the most?
- What is the strangest thing you've ever found in a secondhand store?
- What is the most meaningful antique, old, or inherited item you own? How did you get it?
- What is your favorite era for fashion? If you could have been born in any time period in history, what would it be?

LEVEL UP

To level up this date, plan a full-day excursion to an area you haven't explored and search for more great finds. Enjoy lunch and create a fashion show at home showing off your new duds to one another. If your city hosts a seasonal fashion week, check that out with your partner as well.

SCOOT SCOOT BEEP BEEP

In a play on Donna Summer's lyrics in the 1970s song "Bad Girls," you and your partner will "beep and scoot" through town on bikes or scooters.

MAKE A PLAN

- With most cities offering pickup-and-drop-off bike and scooter rentals, this date requires minimal effort, particularly if you already own your own bikes or scooters.

- Choose your biking/scooting destination and start beeping through the city, boardwalks, bike trails, or sidewalks in your town.

- If you've rented bikes or scooters, be sure to map out your route so you're back in enough time to return them.

- Pack a lunch for two and picnic at a park or trail, or stop off at a nearby restaurant.

START A CONVERSATION

- If you could ride a bike and tour any place in the world, what town or country would you choose?

- When does your partner make you feel the best?

- Name a couple that inspires you.

- What do you admire most about your partner?

LEVEL UP

Imagine biking through France, Switzerland, San Francisco, or the Napa Valley. Take this romantic and relaxing pastime up a notch and plan your next vacation to one of the top domestic or international biking destinations. Or, if you want to save money, consider joining a cycling club or spin class together.

SCULPT YOUR LOVE

Remember the scene in the movie *Ghost* when Patrick Swayze and Demi Moore created pottery together? Pretty romantic. For this activity, sculpt your love together in a pottery-making class.

MAKE A PLAN

- Locate a pottery class in your area and reserve passes. Search online for special offers. Classes may run an hour or two.
- Wear clothes and shoes that can get dirty.
- Think of creative ways to express your love as you sculpt.
- Try breathing in synchronicity with your partner. See if you can allow your hands to relax and move in rhythm.

START A CONVERSATION

- If you could choose to be either an accomplished painter or a sculptor, which would you choose and why?
- Describe the most romantic movie moment you've ever seen.
- How can you express physical intimacy without touching or speaking to one another?
- Imagine breathing onto your partner's neck (as Patrick Swayze does to Demi Moore in *Ghost*). If your partner were a scent, what would they be?

LEVEL UP

Enhance this romantic experience by visiting a sculpting exhibit at a local museum. You can also take a virtual tour of a museum using Google's Arts and Culture application on your smart device. Many museums also offer their own apps and virtual tours as well. If you enjoyed making pottery together, you and your partner can make this a regular date at home using a DIY pottery kit.

READY, "PET," GO

Tap into your inner child and spend the day with animals. Go bird-watching, or visit a pet store or animal shelter and give some love to the animals.

MAKE A PLAN

- This date won't cost anything except an afternoon of your time, attention, and affection.
- Research the best areas to bird-watch. Don't forget binoculars! If you live in a rural area, find a farm with livestock animals that is open to the public.
- The USDA suggests feeding wild animals can be harmful to them, so leave the treats at home.
- If you don't live near a park, visit a pet store or animal shelter and bond with the puppies or kittens.

START A CONVERSATION

- What is your favorite animal? Your least favorite animal?
- Which animal would you least like to meet face-to-face?
- Did you have a pet as a child? What was its impact on your life and your family's life?
- What are your views on domesticated animals? Which ones shouldn't be domesticated?
- What is your strongest childhood memory involving an animal?

LEVEL UP

You can take this date a step further by planning a trip to your local zoo or aquarium. Search online for deals. If you're not a proponent of controlled animal parks, take a much bigger leap with this date and plan a safari, locally or internationally, or visit a national park and observe animals in their natural habitat.

BOATS, PLANES, TRAINS, AND AUTOMOBILES

This activity is like "people watching," but you'll be spectators of transportation instead. Watch planes take off overhead at an airport, relax by the water watching boats come in and out of a seaport, see trains pass, or simply watch cars from a scenic overpass.

MAKE A PLAN

- Try to surprise your partner with this one. This may seem like a "cheap" date, but when you take your partner to a hidden romantic spot they've never experienced, you'll score big points.

- Check the train or airport schedules and marina locations, or find a picturesque spot to "car watch." There may even be a military base nearby where you can observe airplanes (though check ahead of time to make sure you're allowed to visit).

- Pack a lunch or grab takeout and some good background music.

- Keep the location a surprise. As you arrive, when your partner looks at you, bewildered, bring out the food and music, and welcome them to their date.

- Enjoy conversation as you observe the planes, trains, or automobiles. Sitting on the roof of a car can enhance this date significantly.

START A CONVERSATION

- What is the farthest from home you've ever traveled?

- Do you prefer planes, trains, boats, or automobiles as a mode for traveling? If there are any of these you haven't experienced, which would you most like to try?

- What was the most memorable trip you took growing up? Where did you go and how did you travel there?

- Describe the *worst* car ride/plane ride/boat trip you've ever taken.

- Would you rather go to space on a spacecraft or to the ocean's floor in a submarine?

- If you could transport back in time before cars existed, what time period would you choose? How would you travel?

- If the two of you could plan any type of vacation and money was unlimited, where would you go and how would you get there?

- In what ways do you think technology will change travel in the future?

- If you could take a road trip anywhere in the country, what region would you want to travel through? What would you want to see?

LEVEL UP

Level up this date using the mode of transportation of your choice. Research passes to an upcoming car or boat show in your area or book a scenic local train ride. If you want to go back in time to a simpler form of travel, plan a couples' horseback riding excursion or carriage ride. If you want to dig deeper into your pockets, plan to travel to a NASCAR race or even the next Grand Prix. Or, for next-level travel, plan a train-hopping experience on bullet trains in Europe or Asia; for even more luxury, explore the Orient Express.

Food Truck Tour, page 55

CHAPTER 4

Instead of Eating at Your Go-To Restaurant . . .

There's often a feeling of intoxication and euphoria in the early stages of dating, known as the "honeymoon phase." We get a rush of dopamine to the brain whenever we're with our partner, and it feels really, really good. However, over time we settle in and become comfy in the relationship. The familiarity and habituation of being in the relationship occurs, and we stop feeling the novelty we did in the early stages. We may plan fewer romantic dinners and rendezvous, and the desire to impress and turn on our partners may ebb. We may start frequenting the same go-to spots that require minimal effort and time, which results in minimal enthusiasm.

But whether you're looking to bring back the excitement into your relationship after years of dating or you're in a new relationship and want to maintain the thrill, according to psychologist Dr. Chivonna Childs, it's important to go back to what you did in the beginning. Get dressed up, try new things and new restaurants, and be intentional. It's not about spending a lot of money but making your time together special. Childs advises, "[Even] if you're married for 30 years, you should still be dating each other."

The dates in this section shake up the monotony of that same old take-out spot and offer you simple, fun, and exciting ways to bring freshness back into the culinary aspects of your relationship. Each date requires some thought, which can impress your partner, increase teamwork in your partnership, and improve your relationship overall.

AT-HOME RECIPE TAG TEAM

Dinnertime doesn't have to be mundane. Tonight, you're going to build a delicious (or not!), collaborative, and spontaneous meal together. Use your imagination and let your creativity bring the fun.

MAKE A PLAN

- Set a time and date to meet in the kitchen—no planning the meal in advance.
- The first partner chooses one ingredient to begin the recipe (a vegetable, starch, meat, or any food of substance) and prepares it.
- The second partner adds one ingredient to the dish (spices count).
- Alternate until no more than 10 ingredients are used.
- Prepare the table, sit, and enjoy your creation together.

START A CONVERSATION

- Do either of you have food allergies? If you're newly dating, now's the time to discuss them!
- What were your favorite foods as a child? How have your tastes changed?
- Do you have any favorite foods from your cultural heritage and/or do you know how to cook them? Which are most meaningful to you?
- If your partner were a vegetable, which one would they be?
- Think of a name for your recipe. Would you make it again?

LEVEL UP

Take this date to the next level by putting together a recipe cookbook that includes meals you've created together, and share it as a holiday gift for family and other couples.

NOT YOUR AVERAGE TAKE-OUT NIGHT

Tonight's activity is the perfect date to explore and discuss culinary cultural differences. Choose a culturally themed movie or a foreign film and grab takeout with food from that region, or prepare it at home.

MAKE A PLAN

- Choose a film in advance whose culture is different from both of your own.
- Create a menu to cook together that focuses on the film's culture, or find a restaurant to order from.

START A CONVERSATION

- Tell your partner about your cultural heritage and your family of origin. What are some of your favorite traditions and customs?
- How can each of you enhance your knowledge of your partner's heritage and incorporate it into your relationship?
- What are some ways you, as a couple, can increase your knowledge of cultures that you don't share?
- What is your favorite cultural cuisine not connected to your own heritage?

LEVEL UP

Ready to take this date to the next level? Take a foreign language class together, either online or at a local language school. Plan your next vacation to one of your favorite cultural destinations or take a virtual staycation embodying the local sights, sounds, and foods of a particular culture. Check out different cultural restaurants, free museums and galleries, theaters, or art, music, or fashion exhibits in your area.

TAKE A VIRTUAL COOKING CLASS

Ready to take your cooking skills to the next level and learn a specialty cuisine? Tonight, you will scour YouTube for a virtual couples' cooking class or register online for a live virtual cooking class.

MAKE A PLAN

- Choose a specialty cuisine, like sushi, street tacos, or traditional Southern cuisine, or find something basic you've always wanted to try making. Then search for a virtual class online.
- Take turns participating in the meal preparation.
- Put on some background music and enjoy a candlelit dinner together.

START A CONVERSATION

- What was your favorite part of the cooking experience? Your least favorite?
- Do you think the two of you share equitable cooking duties, especially if you share a home? Which of you is the better cook?
- Who was the best cook in your family growing up? What kinds of meals did they make?
- Do you ever feel anxious cooking or choosing a restaurant for your dates?
- If you had to choose one dish to have as your last meal, what would it be?

LEVEL UP

Take this date further and enroll in an in-person cooking class. Search for discount offers online for a variety of couples' cooking classes. Or if you want to keep it at home, purchase a specialty cuisine cookbook and try a new recipe together each month.

DINNER'S "ON YOU" TONIGHT

Tonight, instead of the usual go-to dinner spot, dinner is literally "on you." Level up the romance by surprising your partner with some of their favorite foods placed on your body.

MAKE A PLAN

- Choose a time and date to surprise your partner with this sexy and romantic meal.

- Decide what you'll cook or plan to order takeout. Finger foods (served warm or room temperature) work best. No hot soup! Desserts are also a great option.

- Before your partner arrives, prepare the foods and place them (safely) over your body, wearing either your full birthday suit or a partial one. Be sure your partner knows what time to be there.

START A CONVERSATION

- If you were the one surprising your partner, how did it feel to be vulnerable and physically and emotionally exposed?

- What are some other ways you can express physical vulnerability in your relationship?

- If you weren't the one planning the date, how did you like being surprised?

- Would you rather be the giver or the recipient of intimate surprises?

LEVEL UP

Level up this date with an intimate night of discussing your individual pleasures. Pleasure isn't just related to sexual intimacy. There is also pleasure when our senses are ignited. Spend an evening sharing with one another your favorite tastes, smells and scents, touches, sights, and sounds—whatever moves you and stirs your soul. This is a powerful exercise to get to know your partner more fully, even if you've been together for years.

FOOD TRUCK TOUR

Food trucks are an easy way to taste a multitude of cuisines at a fraction of the cost. On this date, you'll satiate your palates while taking a walk and getting your hearts pumping.

MAKE A PLAN

- Map out your food truck tour before the date. You'll need a small budget, but less than you'd spend at a high-end restaurant.

- Food trucks often cluster in downtown sectors and business districts, but many are also found in suburban areas.

- Consider visiting food trucks with cuisines you've never tasted before.

START A CONVERSATION

- Which food did you like the most today? Was it a new experience or an old favorite?

- What food textures do you prefer? Crunchy, nutty, soft, or smooth?

- If you could only eat one kind of cuisine for the rest of your life, what would it be?

- Which food from today would you like to learn to cook and add to your couples' recipe repertoire?

LEVEL UP

If you'd like to further indulge your palate, level up this date by attending a local food festival. Food festivals, which can also include beer and wine festivals, are fun and adventurous ways to get a taste of different cuisines without getting on an airplane. If you can't find one in your town, it's worth making a drive to a nearby town and creating a new and different outdoor experience for you and your partner. Grab a few friends to join you.

YOU'RE ALL IN MY BBQ GRILL

Ditch the oven tonight and take dinner to the grill. You're grilling homemade kebabs and veggies for you and your sweetie. Don't have an outdoor grill? An indoor grill will work, too.

MAKE A PLAN

- If you don't own a grill, find a used one online or at a yard sale.

- Kebabs can be made with vegetables, steak, lamb, chicken, pork, or fish/shellfish. Pair with easy sides like roasted corn, salads, or grilled vegetables.

- Bring the sizzle of summer, even if it's not summer. Chop up your foods to great music and a refreshing beverage.

- Dine al fresco. If you don't have outdoor space, pack up the food and head to a nearby park.

- If you're grilling in the winter months, turn your television to a tropical setting screensaver and mentally transport yourselves to the beach.

START A CONVERSATION

- What is your favorite season of the year?

- Which season best describes your personality?

- Do you prefer veggies or meat? Fruits or vegetables?

- Did your family have cookouts or dinner parties when you were a child? Who hosted the best ones?

LEVEL UP

Cookouts are a fun and easy way to bring people together. Level up this date by planning a group potluck barbecue or dinner party. If this date made you crave summer and the beach, go extra big with this leveled-up date: Plan a tropical vacation and sip mai tais on the sand.

DINNER IN A DIFFERENT ZIP CODE

This date is simple but still breaks the monotony of your go-to restaurant. Dine at a new and different restaurant. Choose someplace neither of you have visited, maybe even outside your normal travel radius.

MAKE A PLAN

- Search an online restaurant guide for places outside your area that receive rave reviews and book a reservation.
- Or, choose a new place randomly, like spin the bottle—get a map or restaurant guide, close your eyes, and wherever your finger lands is your date-night destination.
- Share your dishes and sample as many different items as you can.

START A CONVERSATION

- How does it feel to intentionally take a risk?
- Did you enjoy trying something new, or do you still prefer your go-to restaurant?
- If you had to travel a little farther than usual, did it feel inconvenient or was it worth it?
- What was your favorite thing about your dining experience tonight?
- Do you feel the need to get out of your relationship comfort zone more often? In what other areas of the relationship can you switch things up?

LEVEL UP

Stay on a roll and level up this date by committing to trying something new in your relationship each month. These dates don't have to be overly thrilling or exorbitant in cost, just new and different. This will enrich your dating life and foster contrasting topics in your conversations.

SIPS AND SWEETS

For today's date, snuggle up with your sweetie on a sofa with a warm beverage and nibble on delectable treats.

MAKE A PLAN

- Select a pastry or coffee shop where you can spend a leisurely and tasty afternoon.

- Try sitting side by side for more physical connection, gentle touches, and affection.

- Order a sampling of different coffees, teas, sweets, and savories.

- Share your treats with your partner and feed one another bites or spoonfuls of dessert.

- Discuss your favorites and least favorites.

START A CONVERSATION

- What was it like to sit side by side? Do you prefer sitting across from one another? Discuss the pros and cons of each.

- Of the desserts you tried, which was your favorite?

- Do you prefer tea or coffee? Decaf or caffeinated? Chocolate or vanilla?

- When it comes to treats, are you more of a sweet or savory person?

- If you had to give up either sweets or coffee/tea for the rest of your life, which would you choose?

LEVEL UP

Keep things sweet with some simple and cost-effective ways to level up this date. Take a pastry class together or bake cookies or other sweets at home and give your treat a signature name that represents your relationship.

BELLIES FULL OF FOOD AND LAUGHS

According to a 2015 *Time* magazine article, couples who laugh together have stronger relationships. For today's date, enjoy an at-home meal together as you stream a stand-up comedy special, and bring pleasure to your bellies with good food and laughter.

MAKE A PLAN

- Choose dinner, whether it's takeout from your go-to spot, a new place you've never tried, or a favorite recipe to cook together.
- Pick a comedy special from a streaming platform or watch snippets of your favorite comedians on YouTube.
- Silence your phones. Eliminate distractions from kids or pets.
- Breathe, relax, and give yourself permission to have fun and laugh so hard that your bellies hurt.
- See who can laugh the loudest.

START A CONVERSATION

- What was your favorite joke of the night?
- What is the funniest joke you've heard?
- Can you create your own funny joke?
- Think about a time in your relationship when you remember laughing together the most. What was happening at the time?
- How can you bring more laughter regularly into your relationship?
- What is your favorite kind of comedy? Slapstick? Sarcasm? Dry humor? Impressions?

LEVEL UP

Keep the laughs going and level up this date with tickets to a live stand-up comedy show. Take advantage of special offers on discount sites. Want to expand the laughter? Invite others to join you for a show or have comedy night at home with food and friends.

DIY FOOD KIT

This activity spruces up your average meal and dining-out experience with a preplanned food kit. There are several affordable food delivery kits found online that are dedicated to special date nights.

MAKE A PLAN

- This date requires minimal effort and is perfect for when you not only want to try something new but also desire a low-key evening. A lot of the work is already done for you in these kits, which list prep and cooking times. Just set a budget, order in advance, prepare as directed, and serve.

- Research your preferred DIY food kit experience. You can choose based on cuisine, prep time, or level of cooking complexity. If you don't fancy a dinner meal, there are also delivery baking kits.

- Plating food is a culinary skill, so try to make it pretty! Take a picture of your final product and compare your finished result with the kit's demonstration photo.

START A CONVERSATION

- What's a favorite meal that your partner could prepare for you?

- What do you like most about cooking together? The least?

- What is the most exciting adventure you've experienced together? And the least exciting?

LEVEL UP

Try a subscription to a regular food kit delivery. There are also some really entertaining and creative date-night boxes you can subscribe to online. Or consider taking an online or in-person plating course together.

IT'S A RESTAURANT KIND OF WEEK

This day date with your special person is a weeklong foodie date. Share a meal at as many different restaurants as you can during a local "restaurant week" or food festival.

MAKE A PLAN

- Investigate your area for restaurant-week dates, locations, and special deals, and book as many places as fit your budget. Book early—spaces during these types of events are filled quickly.

- Discuss and decide with your partner the restaurants and cuisines you'd like to explore. You can take turns choosing or agree on each one.

- Seek out that restaurant you've always wanted to try but never have. Restaurant weeks are a great opportunity to enjoy upscale meals at tremendous discounts.

- If a different restaurant each day is a stretch on the budget, consider lunch or brunch offerings.

- Without being too impulsive or impractical, treat yourself! We all deserve a little splurge from time to time.

START A CONVERSATION

- Do you prefer dining out or eating in?

- If you could have a private dinner prepared by any chef or restaurant in your home, which would you choose?

- Imagine you're a chef at a Michelin Star restaurant. What's your signature dish?

- If you could have unlimited money, power, beauty, or knowledge, which would you choose? Why?

- If you could create five different lives for yourself, what would they look like? How closely does your current life resemble your dream life?

- If you won a million dollars, how would you spend it? Would you collect all your winnings up front or spread them out over time?

- If the apocalypse were tomorrow, how would you spend your last day and with whom?

- If you could reinvent yourself today, who would you be?

Turn up the heat in your own kitchen and recreate this date at home. Pretend you and your partner are both Michelin Star chefs at five-star restaurants for this level-up experience. Bring out the white tablecloth, dinner napkins, candles, and wine, and create a master signature dish together by following either an online recipe or cookbook. Serve a first-class, five-star romantic dinner at home. You can even dress up a bit and put on some classical or jazz music to create the right ambiance.

Sips and Sweets, page 58

Wine-Pairing Class, page 68

CHAPTER 5

Instead of Drinks at Your Local Bar . . .

Are you tired of going to the same old bar with your partner and waking up the next morning feeling that the previous night was pretty uneventful? Well, this section of the book provides alternatives to the clichéd "drinks at a bar" date—ideas that are fun, interesting, and encourage the spark and connection between you and your partner.

On his website MarsVenus.com, Dr. John Gray notes that having drinks together can help make your outings fun and relaxed, but that heightened emotions can also increase conflict. The dates here do often involve alcohol, but with added adventure, imagination, and playfulness—fresh alternatives to frequenting the same old spot with your partner. Nonalcoholic drinks can be easily substituted for any of the date ideas in this section and are frequently suggested in lieu of alcohol.

As drinks are often paired with food, these dates also often involve inspired cooking and creating culinary treats with your partner. Whatever the activity, these dates are designed to bring you closer together, promote teamwork, increase bonding, reduce stress, and enhance fun, communication, and conversation.

CHASE THE SUNSET

Tonight's date brings a romance-and-chill kind of vibe as you and your partner grab a bite, sip mocktails, drive, and chase the sunset.

MAKE A PLAN

- Scout out areas with picturesque views of the sunset and map out your drive.
- Pack a picnic or grab easy takeout with some nonalcoholic beverages.
- Choose your music or make a playlist of meaningful songs for enjoying the sunset.
- If you're newly dating, enjoy the simple pleasures of driving and good conversation. If you've been together a while, enjoy reminiscing about the earlier days of your relationship.

START A CONVERSATION

- Which do you prefer, sunrise or sunset? Are you a morning person or a night person?
- What is the most romantic gesture you've ever made toward a partner?
- What is the most romantic gesture you've ever received from a partner?
- What are some ways you can improve romance in your relationship?

LEVEL UP

Level up this date by intentionally incorporating more romance into your next one. Write a love note to your partner inviting them to a romantic dinner at a surprise location. Get dressed up and make reservations at a new or special restaurant with a gorgeous vista, or enjoy a romantic dinner at home with candles, music, and flowers, followed by a romantic bath for two.

WINE-PAIRING CLASS

Enhance your dining experience by discovering new wine-food pairings, and learn more about your partner's personality by their food and wine preferences. On tonight's date, you'll become top chefs and sommeliers with a virtual wine-pairing class.

MAKE A PLAN

- Research YouTube for a free wine-pairing class or register for a live master class virtual event. You'll need to purchase wines and ingredients in advance.
- Good wine isn't always the most expensive. If your budget is tight, do some homework in advance so you can shop smart.
- Pull out your stemware to pair with the appropriate wines. Thrift shops are a great place to find inexpensive stemware.

START A CONVERSATION

- What was your favorite wine and food pairing? Were there any you disliked?
- If you could be a world-class sommelier or a Michelin-rated chef, which would you choose and why?
- Wine can be transporting; close your eyes and take a sip. Where are you now? What does the taste remind you of?
- What is your favorite hors d'oeuvre at a party?
- Do you prefer red or white wine?

LEVEL UP

Ready to take your new skills further? Plan your next date to an in-person wine pairing or tasting class. Search for special offers. Or, if you're feeling super confident in your new skills, invite friends over and host a wine and hors d'oeuvres cocktail party. If you're feeling a super-big splurge, plan a vacation to a wine country destination, such as the Napa Valley, Bordeaux, Argentina, or South Africa.

BLUES AND BREWS

You don't have to like blues music or beer to enjoy this date. Tonight's focus is on tastes and sounds as you enjoy live music and a drink of your choice for your date night.

MAKE A PLAN

- This date requires time to find a venue where you can listen to live music, and the budget for tickets or a cover charge, if needed. If you want to stay in and save money, livestream a concert at home.

- If you're tempted to hit the dance floor, grab your comfy dance shoes. If you're staying in, transform your living space into a swanky concert hall or bar lounge using candles, lights, or a strobe light.

START A CONVERSATION

- What is your favorite band or type of music?
- Which band/singer do you feel is underrated? Overrated?
- What was the best concert you ever attended?
- What was the worst concert you ever attended?
- You're in a five-member band. Which member are you?
- If you could choose any song in the world that represents who you are, what would it be?

LEVEL UP

Level up this date with a live concert. Find out where your favorite artist is playing and travel to see them perform live, or surprise your partner with tickets to see their favorite artist. Choose from one of the world's famous venues, like the Hollywood Bowl, Red Rocks Amphitheatre, or Madison Square Garden. If travel isn't an option, stream a legendary concert performance from one of the top all-time singers or bands.

PARTY LIKE IT'S 1999

Who says you have to stop clubbing by a certain age? Whether you were born in 1999 or were already a full-fledged adult then, tonight you're going to club it like you're 21.

MAKE A PLAN

- The 20-somethings of any generation would probably say their clubbing was the best of all times. Although this may not be your "clubbing" era, drop your inhibitions and dance the night away in the hottest, trendiest nightclub in your area.

- If trendy isn't your scene, seek out an atmosphere you like or a theme night like '80s night or a disco dance party.

- Establish a jealousy-free zone and discuss the rules of engagement before your date. Can you dance with other people? Is role-playing allowed?

START A CONVERSATION

- What song always gets you on the dance floor?

- What's a song that everyone else loves but you can't stand?

- If you haven't been out dancing in a while (or ever!), what was the experience like? Would you do it again?

- If your ground rules allowed dancing with other people, how did it feel seeing your partner dance with someone else?

- How do you feel about the ground rules you set? Would you handle it differently next time?

LEVEL UP

If you enjoyed your night of dancing and reliving your youth, level up this date by renting a party bus with a group of friends and tour around your city for music, dancing, and fun. For a more affordable option, play a game of "party starters" at the next several events you attend and be the first ones on the dance floor. Get that party started!

MOCKTAIL CONTEST

Instead of going out for libations tonight, stay in and have an alcohol-free night during a mocktail mixology contest. Friends or social media followers can judge your creations.

MAKE A PLAN

- At the grocery store, each partner gets seven minutes to grab supplies (juices, fruits, candies, etc.). Think creatively! Both partners can use all the ingredients.

- At home, each partner gets five minutes to prep their ingredients and five minutes to create their recipe.

- Photograph your concoctions side by side and post on social media, or text family and friends and ask for votes for drink A or B for the most creative and visually appealing mocktail. (Don't let them know who created which mocktail.)

- Best out of three rounds wins! Winner doesn't have to do the dishes for a week.

START A CONVERSATION

- Taste all the mocktails. Which is your favorite?

- If you were a bartender, what would be your signature mocktail/cocktail?

- What was the hardest part about creating your own drink?

- Do you consider yourself creative? Rate your creativity on a scale of 1 to 10. Why did you give yourself that score?

LEVEL UP

Who knew you could have so much fun creating mocktails? Take this date to the next level by inviting friends over to join in the fun. Create teams and keep the creator of each mocktail anonymous to the judges or post on social media and circulate pics for votes. To take it up another notch, enroll in mixology or bartending classes together.

KARAOKE DATE NIGHT AT HOME

Who doesn't love a night of karaoke? Whether you've got singing skills or not, show off your pipes in this noncompetitive night of singing and dancing. Transform your home into a performing stage and let the belting begin!

MAKE A PLAN

- Prepare a playlist of your and your partner's favorite songs to sing. (Instrumentals can also be found easily on YouTube.) Consider adding a few special duets to perform together.

- Rearrange your living space to create a performing stage. Remember, a hairbrush makes a great "microphone" to sing into.

- Sing your hearts out!

START A CONVERSATION

- What are your top five favorite songs of all time?

- What is your favorite song lyric? What does that say about who you are and what you value?

- Who is your favorite vocalist?

- If you could perform a duet with any singer, living or deceased, who would it be?

- Do you have "your song" for your relationship? If not, name three possible candidates.

LEVEL UP

Now that you've had the practice run at home, you're ready to level up this date to an in-person karaoke night. Look into karaoke options in your area and enjoy this date with just the two of you, or expand the fun and include other couples and friends.

SIP AND PAINT

For this date, tap into your inner Van Gogh and enjoy a "starry night" of brushstrokes and beverages as you join an in-person sip-and-paint class.

MAKE A PLAN

- Find a sip-and-paint event in your area, or, if painting at home, register for a virtual class and find out what's needed in advance (likely one canvas each and an inexpensive paint palette).
- Set up a place in your home where you can sit side by side and paint together.
- Replace wine sipping with juice sipping, if preferred.

START A CONVERSATION

- How did the alcohol impact your creativity? Did it help or hinder it?
- Did you feel you were able to express your creativity in the class?
- Were you nurtured in creativity as a child? Are you a visual or auditory learner?
- Do you have a favorite artist? If so, describe what affects you most about their work.

LEVEL UP

Level up this date by hosting a sip-and-paint party. You can either host the event at your home or arrange for a private party at a sip-and-paint venue. If you want to connect more deeply and unlock your inner artists and creative visions, consider completing Julia Cameron's 12-week workbook program, *The Artist's Way*, together. You will be astonished by the visions and creativity you can unleash.

CHARCUTERIE ANYONE?

Charcuterie boards—especially elaborate, meal-size ones—are popular these days. If you've already completed the wine-pairing class (page 68), be prepared to experience even more creativity and adventure in the kitchen.

MAKE A PLAN

- You'll need a wooden cutting board or platter and ingredients like cured meats, cheeses, fruits, nuts, dates, figs, olives, roasted peppers, crudités, cornichons, crackers, breads, chutneys, and rémoulades. Use whatever looks delicious!
- Use YouTube videos or a virtual master class to inspire you.
- Feed nibbles to your partner.
- Pour your vino or sparkling water and toast to your fabulous meal!

START A CONVERSATION

- Did you enjoy this experience? Was it fun and inspiring?
- How was the charcuterie board experience different from a typical sit-down dinner or your usual dinners together?
- What is a favorite meal that your partner prepares for you?
- How did you and your partner work together as a team when creating your board?

LEVEL UP

If you're ready to add more excitement to your culinary experiences, take an in-person charcuterie design class and then invite friends over for a charcuterie gathering. Also, although charcuterie didn't originate in Spain, many Spanish tapas dishes resemble the foods on a charcuterie board. Elevate this dating experience with dinner at a traditional Spanish tapas restaurant for further inspiration.

"NEVER HAVE I EVER"

As a young adult, did you ever participate in the drinking game "Never Have I Ever"? Tonight, take it old-school and play this raucous game of honesty.

MAKE A PLAN

- All you'll need for this date is the two of you, your imaginations, and a libation of your choice or a spicy hot sauce to make it a nonalcoholic challenge.
- Decide up front if any types of statements are off limits.
- Have one partner start with the statement, "Never have I ever . . .," and fill in the blank with something they've never done but believe their partner has. If their partner has done it, they have to drink.
- Alternate taking turns.
- The loser calls game when they can't take any more.
- The winner chooses the next movie or television series to watch.

START A CONVERSATION

- What is the wildest thing you've ever done?
- Was there anything that was difficult for you to reveal or to learn about your partner?
- Do you think partners should know everything about each other, or is it okay to keep some secrets to themselves?

LEVEL UP

Take this drinking game to the next level by creating your own DIY bar crawl. Gather a list of bars or lounges and create a map to hit as many as you can. Use public transportation or walk from bar to bar and grab some greasy food afterward at a late-night diner. If you're ditching the alcohol, try a coffee or dessert crawl instead.

VISIT A FARMERS MARKET

Today's daytime date might be seasonal depending on your area, but many cities have farmers markets that offer different produce during different times of the year. For this easy outing, visit a farmers market and prepare a meal with your bounty of fruits and veggies.

MAKE A PLAN

- This date requires time for you to shop a farmers market and prepare a meal at home using your fruits, vegetables, and other products.

- You can create a recipe from scratch or find one online, but this activity uses a "catch and cook" concept—whichever foods you find at the market, you'll pick and prepare.

- Arrive early and bring a bag for your produce. You may also need to have cash on hand.

- Different foods are available at different times of the year, so research in advance if you're craving something specific.

- Use all your senses to see, smell, touch, hear (tap on the fruits/vegetables), and taste (where samples are offered) the different foods.

START A CONVERSATION

- What was the most unusual food item you saw today?

- Do you think it's worth the extra effort/cost to shop local or organic? Why or why not?

- Have you ever spent time on a farm or working in a garden? What kind of impact did/does it have on you? Share with your partner.

- Do you find it fun or stressful to shop without a plan?

- How important are mutual dietary preferences to you in a relationship?

- Have you ever dated someone who had different food preferences from you? What was your experience like?
- If you're not already, have you ever considered becoming a vegan or vegetarian?
- If you're already a vegetarian or vegan, is there any food you miss eating?
- Name one fruit and one vegetable you've never tried.
- What is your least favorite fruit or vegetable?
- Can you name five fruits that are commonly mistaken for vegetables? Google the answer together.

LEVEL UP

If you enjoyed your farmers market experience exploring Mother Nature's abundance, take this date to the next level by planning a trip to an orchard for apple picking, visiting a pumpkin patch, or enjoying another local bit of agriculture tourism. If those aren't readily available in your area, plan a day-trip date to a nearby farm, if possible. Spend time learning about farming and agriculture, and shop your local farm stand. If you'd like to take your green thumb further, start your own vegetable garden together, or grow fresh veggies and herbs in a planter if there's no space for a garden. Make a point of using your own produce in as many weekly meals as possible.

Scary Movie Night, page 85

CHAPTER 6

Instead of a Ho-Hum Double Date . . .

I f you are newly dating, double dates can be a great way to get to know your partner better and introduce them to your family and friends. And, if you've been together for years, building new double-dating experiences is a fun way to reconnect with old and new friends. It will also introduce different activities into your relationship that will reignite the sparks of fun, adventure, and laughter.

But finding couples to double-date with can sometimes be more challenging than finding a single playdate for a child. Double dates can be a bit more complicated because they require ensuring compatibility, connection, and fun for four different people. Yikes! The best way to approach and plan a group date is to think expansively and create an activity that is fun and engaging for everyone and opens up different topics of conversation. Find common interests and try to choose an activity that will include everyone, so no one feels alienated or bored.

And don't always limit yourself to peers or the same "go-to" couple—double dates can be great (and more interesting) with couples of different ages and backgrounds, especially if you don't usually spend much time outside your own peer group. There's much to learn from one another.

EVERYBODY FONDUE TONIGHT!

If you enjoy having other couples over for dinner but don't always know what to prepare, this is a simple, fun, and engaging alternative to a traditional dinner party. Tonight, you and your partner will create a DIY fondue experience and invite another couple to join you.

MAKE A PLAN

- Follow a YouTube video, online recipe, or cookbook for a complete fondue creation. Decide which cheeses (or vegan options) you'll prepare and their accompaniments, including breads, vegetables, and meats.

- If you're preparing a sweet fondue for dessert, like chocolate, you can serve it with fruit bites like strawberries, pineapple, or peaches.

- Set the ambience with music, lighting, candles, and wine.

START A CONVERSATION

- In your opinion, what is the most fascinating current pop culture trend?

- Which social media platform do you prefer and why? Which site, if any, do you wish you used less?

- What was the most compelling nonpolitical current event you learned of this week?

- What song has been stuck in your head this week?

- What was the last book you read?

- Which app do you spend the most time using?

LEVEL UP

Level up this date with an in-person double date cooking class or cheese- or chocolate-tasting experience for the whole group. Vote on a cuisine that everyone would like to experience and find a local cooking/tasting class.

GROUP KICKBALL GAME

Gather a group of coupled friends and meet up for an evening game of kickball. Bring the coolers and create laughs with this childhood favorite.

MAKE A PLAN

- Locate a spot for your kickball game. Check for reservation fees. Equipment is minimal—all you'll need is an inflatable ball and items to designate as bases, such as cardboard or a base set.
- Invite your other coupled friends to join you. Try to get an even number of team players.
- Have the players bring snacks to share, or plan to grill afterward.
- Divide into teams and choose captains.
- Snap photos to capture the energy and playfulness of the night.

START A CONVERSATION

- What do you think is the best major-league sport: football, baseball, basketball, hockey, or soccer?
- What was your favorite sport in school? Did you play a varsity sport?
- Describe your best memory from childhood involving sports or games.
- Who do you think are the top five greatest athletes of all time, living or dead?

LEVEL UP

Did this date stir up a lot of fun and nostalgia? Happy lives require intentionality and commitment in creating happy memories. Take this date a step further and make the kickball game an annual couple and family daytime event. Bring the kids, parents, and fur babies, and create a family activity that's fun for everyone. You can also level up this date by planning a couples' spectator sport date night. Plan to see your closest professional basketball, football, baseball, or hockey team, or all of you consider joining a local intramural sports team.

OLD-SCHOOL HOUSE PARTY

Hip-hop hooray! Whether you prefer hip-hop, soul, rock, punk, EDM, or pop, tonight's couples' date is a fun, old-school house party. Think teenage dance party, as depicted in many '80s and '90s movie hits, except without the teenage faux pas.

MAKE A PLAN

- For this rager, you can keep it simple and economical. Remember high school, when no one really had their own money? Well, don't break the bank—offer light snacks and BYOB.
- Book a deejay or build a playlist with your favorite dance songs.
- Create space in your home for the dance floor.
- Add some strobe lighting or a red or blue light bulb to your regular light fixture.

START A CONVERSATION

- What was your favorite song of the night?
- What was the best moment?
- Who was the best dancer? Worst dancer?
- What was your worst party experience growing up?
- Did you have fun, and would you do this again? Would you rather host or attend?

LEVEL UP

If you enjoyed hosting a house party, take this fun date night up a notch and host a themed party, such as the next couples' Valentine's Day party, Halloween bash, or New Year's celebration. Search online for inspiration and ideas to make your next themed party a great success.

COUPLES' COOKING CONTEST

Tonight's "dinner-ish" party is a cooking contest between couples. Choose the same dish for each couple to prepare in advance, and on the night of the dinner contest, each person will vote and choose the best dish. Recipes are permitted.

MAKE A PLAN

- Prior to the date, let your guests know the dish for the contest and the rules. Check for food allergies and dietary restrictions.
- Dishes might include: chilis, soups (chilled or hot), the most unusual street taco, or a dessert.
- Give each couple a place card with the name of their dish and a corresponding number.
- Each couple will taste and vote for their favorites.

START A CONVERSATION

- Do you think we chose the best dish to prepare for the contest? Can we improve it for another time?
- Which dish was the most creative? The most original? Which had the best presentation?
- Which did you vote for as number one?
- If you could eat only one person's cooking for the rest of your life, whose would it be?

LEVEL UP

If you enjoyed hosting a dinner party contest, take this date to the next level by hosting an *Iron Chef*–style team cooking contest, which will feature select secret ingredients to prepare the dishes. Place guests on separate teams and have each team prepare a dish using only the ingredients provided and within a specified amount of time. Choose individuals to judge each team's creation based on taste, creativity, presentation, and teamwork.

SCARY MOVIE NIGHT

What do Freddy Krueger, Michael Myers, and Hannibal Lecter all have in common? They may be some of the infamous villains in the movies for your couples' date night tonight. Pull out the scary movie classics for some spookiness and laughs.

MAKE A PLAN

- Invite your favorite couples to join you and choose two scary movies for the night.
- Pop popcorn and prepare other light snacks and drinks. If you want to keep costs down, create a potluck-style experience.
- To create a little more fright, add some spooky lights and Halloween decorations. You can also encourage everyone to wear spooky costumes.

START A CONVERSATION

- What is your favorite scary movie?
- Who do you think is the most terrifying scary-movie villain?
- What is the scariest moment you've experienced in your life? How has it impacted you?
- Does anyone have a good ghost story?
- Would you rather be lost alone at night in the woods or the mountains?

LEVEL UP

If this date didn't scare you away, level it up by planning the next couples' Halloween outing to a corn maze, a haunted house, or an escape room. Or create a DIY escape room or haunted house at home for your next Halloween celebration. Find and follow guidelines on YouTube for an unforgettable night of fear and fright.

A DATE WITH MINIATURE GOLF

For this activity, schedule a night of miniature golf with your coupled friends for some fun and healthy competition.

MAKE A PLAN

- Invite one to two other couples to join you, reserve your spots, and arrange to meet up.
- Choose teams for each event. Losers buy the drinks or dessert afterward.
- If there's no mini-golf in your area, consider a drive to a nearby town or find a go-kart track or arcade for alternative fun and competition.

START A CONVERSATION

- If you could be a world-class, famous golfer or race car driver, which would you choose?
- Would you rather play professional golf or miniature golf?
- What is the greatest adrenaline rush you've experienced?
- What is the one daring adventure activity you would never do? Which one would you like to try the most?

LEVEL UP

Choose your favorite couples and plan a couples' day at a golf tournament. Even if watching golf isn't your thing, it's worth experiencing a new and different event. If you're feeling confident in your skills, create your own couples' golf tournament. You can even charge a token registration fee and donate the profits to charity.

SLUMBER PARTY

Who says sleepovers are only for kids? For tonight's group date, you and your coupled friends will gather at your place for a game and sleepover night full of connection and fun.

- Plan your dinner and breakfast menus, or keep it simple and order pizza, which also makes a great breakfast the morning after.
- Ask each couple to bring their favorite board games.
- Games like charades, Scattergories, Taboo, "Marshmallows and Spaghetti," and Cards against Humanity are easy and fun ways to connect, challenge your brains, get your creative juices flowing, and leave you laughing hysterically.
- If you don't have adequate space for everyone to sleep inside your home, but have a backyard, consider an outdoor camping sleepover.

START A CONVERSATION

- What is your greatest life's purpose you hope to fulfill?
- When you were a kid, what did you want to be when you grew up?
- Who was your biggest school crush?
- Did you ever have a crush on one of your teachers?
- If you came back in another life, who or what would you choose to come back as?
- For which celebrity would you ask your partner to give you a "free pass"?

LEVEL UP

Take this couples' sleepover a step further and plan a couples' camping trip with a few of your favorite couples. Plan activities such as hiking, water sports if they're available to you, and sitting by the campfire with stories and songs.

COUPLES' PAINTBALL

This date comes with a disclaimer: Practice safety and good judgment when playing this game. Now, are you ready? For tonight's date, you and your friends are playing paintball.

MAKE A PLAN

- Find a paintball arena and invite some other couples and friends to join in the fun.
- Be sure to wear protective gear and eyewear.
- Play on teams or as individuals.
- The winner chooses the place for dinner afterward.

START A CONVERSATION

- Was this your first time paintballing and did you enjoy it?
- What was the scariest moment for you?
- Who did you think was going to win prior to the game and why?
- Do you and your partner play better on a team together or solo and why?
- Who is most competitive in your partnership?
- Are you a "good" loser, or is losing hard for you?

LEVEL UP

The bright array of colors in paintball may spark your interest in exploring more with color. Beginning in late February, search your local area for events relating to the Hindu holiday Holi, the festival of colors that marks the end of winter and the start of spring. Holi is celebrated by throwing colored water and powders on each other in merry celebration, and many cities across the country host events. During the winter holidays, you can also enjoy a double date night out viewing a festival of lights.

BELLINIS AND BRUNCH

Instead of meeting the same couple at the same restaurant at the same usual time, switch up couples' dinner night with an afternoon brunch. Incorporate a few simple brunch games to enhance the fun.

MAKE A PLAN

- Make your guest list. Consider including your go-to couples as well as new couples you've spent less time with.

- Make reservations at a new restaurant. Maybe one that offers complimentary mimosas or Bellinis.

- Play a couple of easy table games, like "Who Am I?" where guests guess the names of celebrities and famous and infamous people, and "Two Truths and One Lie," which doesn't require any preparation or tools.

- Arrange for guests to sit next to anyone except their partner—maybe someone they don't know. This will create opportunities for new conversations and connections.

START A CONVERSATION

- Play "Two Truths and One Lie." Each guest will take a turn making two true statements and one false statement about themselves. The other guests must guess which is the lie and write down their answers. Tally scores at the end.

- Play "Who Am I?" Write the names of different celebrities and well-known figures on sticky notes and place them in a bowl. Each guest draws a name without looking and posts it on their forehead for others to see. Each person must ask yes-or-no questions until they successfully guess the celebrity on their sticky note.

- Who are your favorite notable figures in art, literature, music, philanthropy, history, entertainment, science, technology, or sports?

- What new thing did you discover about the people next to you at brunch?
- What is your biggest "lie" that you wish were true about you?

LEVEL UP

Level up this date by bringing the festivities to your home and hosting an afternoon couples' brunch with food and games or a themed brunch, such as a pajama party brunch, an egg or omelet bar, a waffle bar brunch, a holiday brunch, or an outdoor winter brunch. Research simple and popular brunch menu ideas and cocktails or mocktails. Find inexpensive items at a thrift shop to decorate and accent your table with fresh flowers. Plan additional games, like "Forbidden Words," with words that are forbidden for each person to speak during the brunch.

Couples' Paintball, page 88

Love Genie in a Bottle, page 102

CHAPTER 7

Instead of Just Going to Bed . . .

Creating bedtime dates and rituals together with your partner is an important aspect of strengthening physical and emotional intimacy within your relationship. Instead of bedtime being a passive experience, the pre-bedtime dating ideas in this section will create more connection and passion with your partner. According to Dr. Michelle Drouin, "Sex or no sex, going to bed as a couple is a gateway to increased connection. At the end of the night, unencumbered by children, work tasks, and housework, people can really unwind. They can talk and touch. Just being in the bedroom at nighttime with a partner is a promising concoction for intimacy." The dates within this chapter allow you the opportunity to be very intentional with this special time together at the end of each day.

These dates are also designed to prepare you and your partner for deeper, more restorative sleep. Connecting with your partner before bedtime, not only in a sexual way, increases oxytocin, the "love hormone," which promotes feelings of empathy, trust, and sexual and emotional connection, and decreases anxiety. The Better Sleep Council explains that as oxytocin rises we begin to feel calm and protected, which in turn creates feelings of safety and security, allowing us to fall asleep more easily and sleep more deeply.

"BEDITATION" TIME

Couples that meditate together, stay together. Instead of getting into bed and going directly to sleep tonight, you and your partner can try a meditation in bed, also known as a "beditation."

MAKE A PLAN

- All you'll need for this date is each other, your bed, and a smartphone or computer to listen to relaxing meditation music, a guided meditation, or a healing sound bath.

- Find a meditation on YouTube or on an app. For full mind and body relaxation, plan on 20 minutes. If that sounds daunting, start with 10.

- Set the mood for your meditation experience with dimmed lights, candles, and essential oils.

- Sit up side by side on the bed with your shoulders touching, or hold hands to deepen the synergy.

- Focus on your breathing and try to synchronize your breath.

START A CONVERSATION

- Describe your meditation experience.

- Did you enjoy meditating together? Would you like to do it again or make it a part of your nighttime ritual?

- What were some of your predominant thoughts during the meditation?

- Were you able to focus your mind? Where you able to focus on just your breathing?

LEVEL UP

You can level up this date by meditating lightly clothed or naked together, sitting in front of one another in the lotus position, and placing your hand over each other's hearts. You can also join an in-person meditation class or a sound-bath experience (search for one online).

BEDTIME BOOK CLUB

Tonight you'll choose from any book genre and either read from a book or listen to an audiobook. This bedtime date encompasses shared quality time and intellectual intimacy.

MAKE A PLAN

- Flip a coin to see who chooses the book. Purchase a physical copy of the book, download it to an ebook device, or use the audio version; or grab one of your favorites from your own bookshelf.
- You can either snuggle up in bed or on the couch for your reading date.
- Choose the number of chapters to read. You can have each partner take turns reading out loud, read an individual copy of the book separately, or listen together to the audiobook.

START A CONVERSATION

- Did you enjoy the book and the date?
- Discuss the key points of the chapters and share each person's point of view.
- If you're a reader, what kinds of books do you prefer reading? Fiction or nonfiction? Biography? Mystery?
- Whom would you like to write your biography?
- Would you like to continue reading this book together as a nightly date?

LEVEL UP

Take this shared reading experience a step further and create your own couples' book club, reading a book together and discussing it nightly or at a monthly book meeting. You can also choose one of your favorite books for your partner to read and have them do the same. If you'd like to begin reading through a personal development book together, *The Four Agreements* by Don Miguel Ruiz or *The Alchemist* by Paulo Coelho are short and powerful books and a great place to start.

CAN WE TALK?

In the early dating days of your youth, you may have experienced long, giggly, flirty hours chatting on the phone with your crush. If you haven't, give it a try! Spend the evening talking on the phone instead of going to bed.

MAKE A PLAN

- Go into separate rooms and close the door.
- Whoever initiated courtship in your relationship will be the partner that rings up the other one.
- Keep conversation fun, light, and flirty. Remember you're like young adults dating for the first time and getting to know one another.

START A CONVERSATION

- Would you rather have the power to fly or the power to be invisible?
- What are your biggest pet peeves?
- What is your favorite board game?
- If you could have one incredible gift or talent, what would it be?
- Which way does your toilet paper go on the roll?

LEVEL UP

Did you have fun talking with your honey? If so, level up this date by incorporating the phone date into your dating repertoire or commit to a regular habit of talking to one another before bedtime—having "pillow talk" or storytelling without any distractions or interruptions. That means no television, no music, no books, no kids, and no games. Just the two of you sharing true quality time before drifting off to sleep.

SPA NIGHT

Bedtime is made more calming and relaxing with tonight's date as you convert your home into a spa and delight in sensual exploration of one another.

MAKE A PLAN

- Set aside a few hours for your spa night together and purchase your spa supplies in advance. Get creative with candles, soaps, body scrubs, facial masks, essential oils, loofahs, and flowers.
- Start your spa date with a yummy rose-petal bubble bath and a glass of champagne.
- Use specialty soaps and body scrubs to lather one another.
- Follow your bath or steamy shower by applying body oils to one another.
- Give each other sensual body massages. Decide the length of each massage, relax, and sink into tranquility.

START A CONVERSATION

- Did you enjoy spa night? What was your favorite part? What was your least favorite part?
- Do you prefer a Swedish or a deep-tissue massage? If you've never gotten a massage, would you consider one?
- What is your favorite part of your body to be touched?
- What is your least favorite part of your body to be touched? Which parts of your body are off-limits during sexual intimacy?

LEVEL UP

Make your spa night a spa day at a local day spa! Search online for promotional offers for couples' treatments and packages. Look into couples' massages or a couples' mud bath experience. If you want to break the bank, book a spa weekend at a luxurious spa resort or hotel.

HIDE-AND-GO-GET-IT

Tonight's date is an adult twist on a game of hide-and-seek. After you find your partner, you'll request a flirtatious and sexual favor from them, like a warm kiss, a back rub, or a quick make-out session.

MAKE A PLAN

- Establish the rules and boundaries, and places you're allowed to hide. You can even include the outdoors within your hiding parameters.

- Enjoy taking turns hiding from and seeking your partner. Keep it playful, sensual, and fun.

- Ideally, the game ends when you can't take your hands off of each other.

START A CONVERSATION

- Did you prefer being the hider or the seeker?

- What is your favorite sexual favor to give? What is your favorite sexual favor to receive?

- What is the closest thing you possess to a fetish?

- Do you enjoy bringing games into your intimacy? Discuss and come up with other fun games you can play to enhance sexual intimacy.

LEVEL UP

If you and your partner want more fun and games, why not level up this date with a game of strip poker or another card game that entails sensual fun and pleasure. For some sheer fun and laughter, play hide-and-seek on your next visit to a grocery store or shopping center.

DIY CANDLE KIT

Imagine creating a candle with a scent that embodies your relationship and that, when it burns, ignites deeper chemistry and passion between you. For tonight's date, you and your partner will use a candle kit to create your own "aroma of love."

MAKE A PLAN

- Buy a DIY candle-making kit. To explore additional scents, visit an apothecary shop for essential oil fragrances that most suit your personalities and characterize your relationship.
- Create a mood, including music, candles, dessert, and wine.
- As you build your fragrances, experiment with smell together.
- Take turns smelling a scent with your eyes closed and describing the emotions and experiences evoked with each fragrance.
- The next evening, after the candle wax has settled, light your candle and enjoy the aroma.

START A CONVERSATION

- Which scent was your favorite?
- Do you prefer tropical ocean breeze or earthy, woodsy scents?
- What is your favorite cologne or perfume to wear? Which is your favorite to smell?
- Is there a scent that reminds you of a pleasant or unpleasant memory from your past?
- What's the name of your candle?

LEVEL UP

"Keep to your senses" and level up this date by taking a shopping excursion together to find each of your signature fragrances. Assist one another in choosing a fragrance that you both enjoy. If you want to take this date even deeper, plan to spend a day at a perfumery.

WHAT'S IN THE JAR?

Surprise your partner with a little game before bed with this activity, using only items from your bathroom. Your blindfolded partner will guess what's inside a jar using only their sense of touch and smell. **Warning: Do not use cleaning supplies that are toxic to smell or touch.**

MAKE A PLAN

- You will each choose up to five items from your bathroom. You can use facial creams, hair gels, lotions, bath bombs, facial gel masks, toothpaste—the list is endless.

- Place the items in containers so your partner can touch and smell them.

- Blindfold your partner and let them guess each item. If they're incorrect, rub the item safely over parts of their face or body. If they guess correctly, rub the item over yours.

- Take turns.

- You may need a shower together following this juicy date.

START A CONVERSATION

- If you had to give up one of your senses, which would you choose?

- If you could supercharge one of your senses, which would you choose?

- How did different textures make you feel? Did they feel calming and relaxing or agitating and disturbing?

LEVEL UP

Notice which textures and items felt soothing to you both and plan a date to make homemade meditation and mindfulness tools, such as slime, floam, flubber, play dough, DIY sensory blocks (think LEGO), a glittery meditation jar, a bauble (wrap tape into a ball), or beaded jewelry. Or, plan a date to shop for crystals and meditation balls.

LOVE GENIE IN A BOTTLE

Tonight's date is inspired by an idea from relationship expert Dr. John Gray of MarsVenus.com. For this activity you'll take turns as each other's "love genie in a bottle," granting your partner's desires within a 30-minute time frame.

MAKE A PLAN

- Discuss the rules and parameters for your date.
- Wishes can't be too arduous and must be attainable within the time limit. Some examples might be a foot rub or body massage, folding the laundry, making dessert, or putting the kids to bed.
- Take turns being each other's "genie."
- Set the timer for 30 minutes for each partner's turn and begin fulfilling the other's wishes.

START A CONVERSATION

- What was your least favorite task to do?
- What was your most enjoyable task to do?
- What were your household chores as a child? Did you receive an allowance for completing your chores and if so, how much?
- Who did most of the housework in your home growing up?
- Imagine you have a real genie in a bottle. What are your three wishes?

LEVEL UP

Chores can be more fun if you share them. How about making the mundane task of chores a dating experience of shared quality time? Bring this date up a notch by making a regular household chore a teamwork effort. It could be washing the dishes and cleaning the kitchen together, along with music and conversation, or doing the laundry or the yardwork together. Consider also making the "Love Genie in a Bottle" date part of your normal regimen.

DO A LOVE SCAVENGER HUNT

Today's daytime bonus date is a DIY scavenger hunt played inside your home. You can either (1) create a scavenger hunt with items you and your partner find together, or (2) create a strategic scavenger hunt with clues for your partner to find successive items.

MAKE A PLAN

- You'll need time to plan your scavenger hunt. If you're creating a strategic scavenger hunt, you'll need to write notes with clues and leave them in secret places for your partner. You can also search online for scavenger hunt ideas and printouts.

- If you're creating a strategic scavenger hunt with successive items, choose items and leave notes with clues to lead your partner to the next treasure. Make the last item a surprise lover's gift, like giving them a one-hour massage, making their favorite dinner, or buying tickets to a movie.

- If you're doing a checklist scavenger hunt together, use the list and set a timer for how long you'll each have to search for items. You can also have a theme, such as household items meaningful to you both or items that represent your relationship.

START A CONVERSATION

- Was it too easy or too hard to find the scavenger hunt items?

- What was most difficult about creating the checklist or clues for your partner?

- How do you feel about your partner and your relationship after this activity? Do you feel connected? Appreciated? Exhausted?

- Have you ever snooped through a partner's personal items? Did you find anything that surprised you?

- Should partners share passwords?

- Is privacy important between partners? What should boundaries look like between partners?

- Is there anything you've ever wanted to know about your partner but have been too afraid to ask? Discuss your answers.
- Are you the type of person who likes surprises, or do you like to know what's going on at all times?
- What is the biggest surprise you've ever received from a partner?
- What is the biggest surprise you've ever given to a partner?

LEVEL UP

Take this adventure outside the home and level up your date with a scavenger hunt in a downtown area or park near you. You can search online for printable lists of items to find in either location, or you can create your own checklist together. Map the location in advance and set the length of time for the search. The winner is whoever finds the most items during the allotted time. The loser treats the winner to ice cream at a nearby parlor. Alternatively, for the next birthday or holiday celebration, plan a surprise scavenger hunt for your partner around town and get all your local friends and family in on the fun by leaving clues near or outside their homes.

Spa Night, page 98

Saddle Up, page 111

CHAPTER 8

Instead of Your Typical Weekend Getaway . . .

Though the evidence exists, most of us don't need research to know vacations and relaxing breaks have numerous benefits, including improved mental and physical health, decreased stress and burnout, improved relationships, and greater boosts to happiness. Richard Davidson, professor and founder of the Center for Healthy Minds, suggests that traveling breaks our regular routines and forces us to be more present and mindful.

Today's world is more hyper-paced and stressful than ever, which can put more strain on couples and marriages. Vacations with focused time away are paramount for couples to come back to their everyday relationship with more meaningful quality time, intentionality in prioritizing their relationship, decompression from life's daily stressors, and shared fun and adventure.

Taking regular vacations with a partner may sound daunting if your budget precludes it. But creating a break—of any kind—from your normal routine, as suggested by Davidson, doesn't have to be costly. The dates in this section are not your typical weekend getaways—they're unique, fun, and mindful ideas that allow you and your partner to take a break from monotony and change your scenery but also keep your costs down. Since these getaways involve weekend activities or excursions, you'll find day dates thrown in as well.

BAE-CATION STAYCATION

This weekend, enjoy a bae-cation staycation—a vacation with your bae without leaving your home.

MAKE A PLAN

- Prepare like you're going for an actual getaway. Commit to unplugging from work and your devices for the weekend. Skip the household chores; get a sitter, if necessary; and brainstorm activities for the weekend.

- Plan little touches that make your home feel like a hotel (like leaving warm cookies on your bedside table for the evening's turndown).

- Transform your bathroom into a mini-spa and light candles.

- Use your best dishes and order "room service" from your favorite delivery or take-out restaurant.

- Be tourists in your own town, experiencing hikes, museums, beaches, festivals, and bike rides.

- Cuddle by the fireplace, or make a firepit in your backyard.

- Don't forget breakfast in bed.

START A CONVERSATION

- What do you most look forward to on vacation and why?

- What are five of your greatest accomplishments?

- What is one of your favorite memories of your relationship (even if you've been dating a short time)?

- Imagine you are together in a time machine. Where are you going?

LEVEL UP

Level up this date by planning a staycation outside of your home in your own hometown. Book a hotel, B&B, or vacation home rental like an Airbnb or Vrbo. Plan excursions or stay in all weekend.

COUPLES' HOUSE SWAP WEEKEND

Have you ever seen the movie *The Holiday*, where two women swap homes in each other's countries over the Christmas holiday? Instead of paying for costly flights and hotel rooms, you will swap homes with another couple in your hometown or state.

MAKE A PLAN

- Think of another couple who would be interested in swapping their home for a weekend. Plan your weekend well in advance so that you and your friends can synchronize calendars accordingly and book activities prior to your arrival.

- Plan to have your home hotel-ready for your guests. Offer fresh sheets and towels, and stock basic staples in your kitchen and bathroom. Leave a nice welcoming note and a surprise treat.

- Enjoy activities and adventures popular in the area. Or, if you'd rather stay in all weekend, stock the cupboards, watch movies, and play games.

- Be sure to leave the home the way that you found it!

START A CONVERSATION

- Did you enjoy the couples' house swap, and would you do it again?
- Which cities and countries are on your bucket list to visit and why?
- How many different states in America have you visited? How many different countries?
- What was the best vacation you ever took and why?
- Which traveling experience had the greatest impact on your life?

LEVEL UP

It's time to cross the border and the seas and level up this date with a couples' house swap with friends outside of your state or country. Take advantage of knowing cool people that live in cool places you've never visited.

SADDLE UP

Pull out the denim jeans, flannel shirts, cowboy hats, and boots—you and your honey are going bull riding . . . on a mechanical bull, of course.

MAKE A PLAN

- If you can't find a venue with a mechanical bull in your area, play a virtual bull-riding video game online.
- Grab your jeans and boots and saddle up.
- If you have trouble staying on as you ride, that's okay! Laughing hysterically at one another is half the fun.
- Keep score and see who can stay on the bull the longest. The loser pays for drinks.

START A CONVERSATION

- Was this your first time riding a "bull"? If so, did you enjoy it? If you have ridden before, what was the longest you've been able to ride?
- Have you ever visited Pamplona, Spain, and would you ever consider participating in the running of the bulls or watching a bullfight?
- What would it take for you to ride an actual bull?
- Have you ever ridden a horse? Did you enjoy it and why?

LEVEL UP

Enhance this weekend's date by leveling up with a horseback-riding lesson or attend a livestock show or rodeo. Check your city's local guide for activities and festivities. Discuss together your experiences riding horses, who are very intuitive animals with an adroit ability to sense their rider's energy. Share with your partner the type of energy you believe the horse might sense from you.

ENJOY A "LOVEMAKING" FEST!

If you feel there's too much routine in your romance, dedicate this weekend to spontaneity and exploring each other in every room in your home.

MAKE A PLAN

- Set the mood for your love fest using candles, flowers, music, foods, candies, wine, movies, body oils, and rubs.
- Turn off your phones and immerse yourselves in one another.
- This date works well on a rainy or snowy day or during the cooler seasons when you may want to cocoon and be holed up inside.

START A CONVERSATION

- Which was your favorite room for making love and why?
- Do you enjoy more spontaneous sex or scheduled sex?
- Is there a place you've always wanted to have sex and haven't?
- What has been your most awkward experience during sex?
- Where did you learn about sex? Did your parents openly talk about sex when you were growing up? What was their view toward sex?
- If applicable, whom did you lose your virginity to?
- Have you ever accidentally walked in on someone having sex? If so, describe that moment.

LEVEL UP

Level up this date by creating a couple's lovemaking bucket list. Grab a notebook and write down both of your fantasies and dream lovemaking locations (without getting caught—and safety first, of course!). Maybe that looks like outside in the rain or snow, in a swimming pool, in a hot tub, on the beach, in an elevator, in your parents' home, on the kitchen floor, on a piano, or on a staircase. Make a plan to start crossing off items on your bucket list.

GO CAMPING IN YOUR BACKYARD

Ready to try something new and adventurous with your partner? Why not camp in your backyard? It's easy, affordable, and fun.

MAKE A PLAN

- Set up your backyard with tents and prepare a firepit.
- If you don't have a backyard, ask family or friends to use their yard for the weekend, or turn your living room into a campground.
- Most campgrounds have limited access to Wi-Fi, so unplug for the weekend even in your own backyard.
- Make s'mores and sing campfire songs.
- Tell each other nighttime stories and gaze up at the stars.

START A CONVERSATION

- Growing up, were your family campers, road-trippers, or jet-setters? Which do you prefer now?
- Did you go to sleepaway camp when you were young? If so, what was your experience like?
- What is your favorite camp song?
- What is your favorite teen camp movie?
- Do you think there's life on other planets?
- Have you ever experienced something supernatural? If so, can you describe what occurred?

LEVEL UP

Take this weekend date a step further and plan a full-on camping excursion at a campground or state park. If you want to dig deeper into your pockets, rent a camper or an RV for the weekend. You can also take your camper on a longer road trip to other popular camping sites.

TAKE A MINI-GETAWAY

This weekend you're taking an actual mini-vacation. Although this might not be your dream destination or an extravagant trip, the idea is to take a break from your typical destination or the same type of vacation and share quality time, relaxation, and fun.

MAKE A PLAN

- Plan your quick getaway, including flights, hotels, vacation rentals, and car rentals, and map out the details. If you need time to budget, plan in advance and start stashing your coins.

- Make plans to visit a new and desirable place from your couple's bucket list. If you typically go to the beach, try the mountains instead. If it's always a laid-back, outdoorsy trip, try a big city.

- Book activities and excursions prior to your arrival, if necessary, or plan a completely spontaneous trip.

START A CONVERSATION

- Are you and your partner compatible travel partners? If yes, what are your strengths and areas of compatibility? If not, where can you improve?

- Getting along on vacation can be more or less challenging than getting along at home. What's been your experience on this trip?

- Name five things you both like doing together on vacation.

LEVEL UP

Imagine making your dream vacation a reality. For this level-up experience, set a date and plan and strategize for your dream vacation. Maybe it's a year or even two years out, but there's no better time than the present to begin planning. Set aside time to discuss and plan regularly for your trip. Search travel magazines and blogs for inspiration in planning your vacation, and make a vision board. Work toward the budget and monthly savings to make your dream vacation a reality.

TAKE A DIP TOGETHER

This weekend's date is seasonal if you live in colder climates, but year-round if you're in sunny weather or have access to an indoor pool. Frills and fun fill this date as you and your partner take a dip in a pool.

MAKE A PLAN

- If you don't have access to a pool at your home or apartment dwelling, scout friends and family or a recreational center where you and your partner can take a dip together.
- Pack your pool bag with your suits, lunch, refreshments, a book, and music, and don't forget the sunscreen if you'll be outside.
- If you have access to a private pool, ditch the swimsuits and enjoy skinny-dipping together.
- Enjoy an old-fashioned game of "Marco Polo" and relax poolside.

START A CONVERSATION

- Have you ever gone skinny-dipping? If so, describe your experience.
- Do you prefer the pool or the beach?
- How old were you when you learned to swim? Who taught you? If you don't know how, are you willing to learn now?

LEVEL UP

Whether you enjoyed swimming or just lounging by the pool, level up this date and take a swim at your local river or lake if it's available to you. Or book a pool day at a local hotel or resort spa. Reserve an all-day pool pass, and if you want to take this date up another notch, rent a cabana. Relax in the sun and enjoy nibbles and libations.

DIY HOME-IMPROVEMENT PROJECT

Maybe you have been putting off a home-improvement project that you keep promising yourself you're going to do. This weekend's date allows time for couple's teamwork as you build a project together.

MAKE A PLAN

- Choose a weekend DIY improvement project you can work on together.
- If you're not feeling handy, try cleaning out a closet or rearranging the living room furniture.
- Set the mood for your project experience with inspiring, energetic music. When you break for the day, enjoy food, conversation, and a relaxing movie.

START A CONVERSATION

- Who was the do-it-yourself fixer in your household growing up?
- Do you recall any favorite building projects from school?
- What is your favorite type of home architecture? Farmhouse? Modern? Tudor? Ranch? Colonial? What kind of building says "home" to you?
- What's the best home you've ever lived in and why?
- If money were no object, what kind of dream home would you build and where?

LEVEL UP

To deepen your building skills and take this date to the next level, sign up for an in-person woodworking class together or create your own decorative DIY hanging wooden board. Find the desired-size piece of wood and paints to color your board. Research different themes for your board, such as a nautical theme, fruits and veggies, or wines. Hang your finished product on the wall of your home or use it as part of a coffee table or end table.

ZIP AND SIP

Adventure and adrenaline pack this weekend's date as you plan a day of zip lining followed by sipping brews on a patio.

MAKE A PLAN

- Locate an outdoor zip-lining adventure in your area or within driving distance. Plan to spend the day outdoors. If you can't find one, research indoor zip-lining options. You can also try another indoor adventure like indoor rock climbing.
- Continue the rush and thrills with lunch and brews after your adventure.

START A CONVERSATION

- Did you enjoy the activity? What were your feelings before embarking on the adventure? Were you nervous? Afraid?
- What is your worst adventure story?
- Would you rather go rock climbing on a mountain or bungee jumping? Or neither?
- What type of adventure would reflect your greatest fear?
- Name three different things that frighten you.
- What was your worst roller-coaster experience?
- Did the adrenaline rush make you more attracted to your partner?

LEVEL UP

There are several ways to level up this date if you and your partner enjoy adventure and taking risks together. You can plan a morning in a hot-air balloon, outdoor rock climbing, or skiing; or, take it to the next level and go skydiving (plan responsibly and safely, of course). Many of these activities can also be planned as part of your next getaway.

A TRIP DOWN MEMORY LANE

For this activity, you will spend the weekend taking a trip down memory lane, reminiscing and visiting all your favorite dating places, and if possible, sharing favorites from your single days.

MAKE A PLAN

- Create a map of your destinations or take a spontaneous trip down memory lane in the town where you were first dating.

- If you're in your childhood town or city (or it's nearby), share memories of your childhood with your partner, like a visit to your elementary or high school, your favorite ice cream parlor, restaurants you frequented when you were single, parks you played in, where you received your first kiss, or where you attended prom.

- Snap photos of you now and compare with photos of you when you first got together.

START A CONVERSATION

- What is your biggest regret from your past? If you could do it over again, what would you change?

- What is one of the most defining moments from your childhood or anytime in your past that made the biggest impact on your personal development and in your life?

- Describe what would have been your ideal family growing up.

- Were the people who raised you strict or lenient growing up?

- Do you think more about the past, the present, or the future?

- What are you most excited for in your future and why?

- What concerns you most about your future and why?

- What makes you feel anxious and uncertain and why?

- Whether you've been together for years or are newly dating, what made you realize your partner was the one you wanted to get to know?

Level up this date and plan a mini-reunion with family, friends, or both. Gather local or long-distance friends for a group dinner party at home or pull out all the stops and plan a full weekend reunion with your out-of-state family or oldest friends from the past. Use resources online to help you plan a reunion weekend of fun and nonstop laughter. You can scout activities, create a budget and itemize costs, then have friends and couples pitch in on food and other expenses.

A Final Note

You did it! If you're reading this final page, then you made your way through the book. Congratulations! I hope that your relationship has experienced a new sense of life and connection. I also hope that in working through this book you garnered loads of new wisdom about your partner, discovered more about yourself, experienced many aha moments, and created lots of fun, wild, and passionate memories.

Dating and healthy relationships, like anything else in our lives, take consistency and commitment. My hope is that when you were completing this book you experienced all of the boons from routinely dating your partner. Maybe not every future date will look just like the ones inside this book, but what's most important is that you and your partner find regular quality time for one another, treating your relationship as a living entity that is prioritized and nurtured properly. Don't let dating end with the end of this book. Commit to having a regular date night with your partner each week. Maintain the spirit of novelty and adventure. Use other online resources, books, podcasts, and videos to keep spawning new dating ideas.

I hope that you will refer back to this book again and again, and that you will share it with other couples whose relationships may need a dose of vigor and inspiration. Good luck on your continued dating journey!

Resources

Books:

The Alchemist by Paulo Coelho

The Artist's Way: A Spiritual Pathway to Higher Creativity by Julia Cameron

Attached: The New Science of Adult Attachment and How It Can Help You Find—and Keep—Love by Amir Levine and Rachel S. F. Heller

Beyond Mars and Venus: Relationship Skills for Today's Complex World by John Gray

Conscious Loving: The Journey to Co-Commitment by Gay Hendricks and Kathlyn Hendricks

The 5 Love Languages: The Secret to Love That Lasts by Gary Chapman

The Four Agreements: A Practical Guide to Personal Freedom by Don Miguel Ruiz

The Secret Method to Conscious Love Workbook Journal by Angela N. Holton

Websites:

Alison Armstrong: AlisonArmstrong.com

Clarence Shuler: ClarenceShulerOnline.com

Crated with Love, Date Boxes: CratedWithLove.com/dateboxes

LGBT Relationship Network: LGBTRelationshipNetwork.org

The Love Language™ Quiz: 5LoveLanguages.com/quizzes/love-language

Rising Woman: RisingWoman.com

Stefanos Sifandos: StefanosSifandos.com

Stephan Speaks: StephanSpeaks.com

Podcast:

The Relationship School: RelationshipSchool.com/relationship-school-podcast

References

Andrews, Arden Fanning. "Why Puzzles Are 2020's Most Surprising Relationship Tools." Free People. Accessed July 14, 2022. freepeople.com/puzzles-in-2020.

Ardeen, Shelly. "Backyard Camping Is an Excellent Alternative to Traditional Camping." The Terra Guide. September 11, 2021. theterraguide.com/activities/backyard-camping-is-an-excellent-alternative-to-traditional-camping.

Basu, Tanya. "Couples Who Do This Together Are Happier." *Time.* August 27, 2015. time.com/4010484/couple-laughing-study.

Better Sleep Council (blog). "The Benefits of Sleeping Together." February 5, 2019. bettersleep.org/blog/the-benefits-of-sleeping-together.

Caldwell, Kim. "How Couples' Meditation Strengthens Relationships." LiveAbout.com. May 23, 2019. liveabout.com/couples-meditation-4177963.

Castrillon, Caroline. 2022. "Why Taking Vacation Time Could Save Your Life." *Forbes Magazine.* November 9, 2022. https://www.forbes.com/sites/carolinecastrillon/2021/05/23/why-taking-vacation-time-could-save-your-life/?sh=4938add924de.

CBS News. "What Your Favorite Movies Say about You." February 5, 2008. cbsnews.com/news/what-your-favorite-movies-say-about-you.

Chapman, Gary D. *The 5 Love Languages: The Secret to Love That Lasts.* Chicago: Northfield Publishing, 1992.

Chatel, Amanda. "When It Comes to Romance, Science Has Good News for Adrenaline Junkies." Mic. February 26, 2015. mic.com/articles/111382/when-it-comes-to-romance-science-has-good-news-for-adrenaline-junkies.

Clemence, Sara. "5 Reasons You Need to Take a Vacation, According to Science." *Travel + Leisure.* Last updated August 13, 2021. travelandleisure.com/trip-ideas/yoga-wellness/why-vacation-matters-the-science-of-taking-time-off.

Cleveland Clinic (blog). "What Is the Honeymoon Phase and How Long Does It Last?" February 3, 2022. health.clevelandclinic.org/what-is-the-honeymoon-phase.

Cronkleton, Emily. "12 Benefits of Cycling, Plus Safety Tips." Healthline. Last modified December 15, 2021. healthline.com/health/fitness-exercise/cycling-benefits.

Dashnaw, Daniel. "5 Reasons Why Date Night Is Important—25 Suggestions." Couples Therapy Inc. Last modified May 13, 2019. couplestherapyinc.com/5-reasons-date-night-important.

Dolan, Eric W. "Romantic Nostalgia Linked to Greater Relationship Commitment, Satisfaction, and Closeness." PsyPost. July 27, 2022. psypost.org/2022/07/romantic-nostalgia-linked-to-greater-relationship-commitment-satisfaction-and-closeness-63593#:~:text=Once%20again%2C%20the%20researchers%20found,those%20in%20the%20control%20condition.

Drouin, Michelle. "Why Partners Should Try to Go to Bed at the Same Time." *Psychology Today*. February 10, 2021. psychologytoday.com/us/blog/love-online/202102/why-partners-should-try-go-bed-the-same-time.

Eddins, Rachel. "Enjoy Some Relationship Fun: Have an 'I Love You' Scavenger Hunt." Eddins Counseling Group. April 24, 2017. eddinscounseling.com/enjoy-relationship-fun-love-scavenger-hunt.

Glass, Lori Jean. "The Importance of Dating in Your Relationship." PIVOT. January 26, 2022. lovetopivot.com/why-dating-important-relationship-building-skills-workshop.

Goldsmith, Barton. "The Importance of Romance." *Psychology Today*. June 3, 2013. psychologytoday.com/us/blog/emotional-fitness/201306/the-importance-romance.

Gray, John. "Alcohol and Relationships: A Recipe for Fighting or a Chance for Intimacy?" MarsVenus.com. Accessed August 3, 2022. marsvenus.com/blog/alcohol-and-relationships.

Hollman, Laurie. "The Importance of Imaginative Play for Kids and Adults." Laurie Hollman, Ph.D. April 19, 2021. lauriehollmanphd.com/2021/04/19/the-importance-of-imaginative-play-for-kids-and-adults.

Holton, Angela N. *The Secret Method to Conscious Love: Deepen Understanding of Yourself and Improve Your Relationships*. 2nd ed. Columbia: Little Kobi Bear, 2021.

Isham, Kathryn. "Importance of Taking a Vacation." Allina Health. June 15, 2021. allinahealth.org/healthysetgo/thrive/importance-of-taking-a-vacation.

Katz, Allan J. "Guide on Building Healthy Intimacy for Couples." Marriage.com. Last modified April 3, 2020. marriage.com/advice/intimacy/building-healthy-intimacy-for-couples.

Kearns, Brad. "John Gray." *Get Over Yourself* podcast. Episode 197. Accessed August 8, 2022. bradkearns.com/2020/07/28/healing -strained-relationships-with-increased-self-awareness-hopeful -new-strategies-and-fake-it-till-you-make-it.

Johnson, Maisha. "How to Understand and Build Intimacy in Every Relationship." Healthline. April 16, 2019. healthline.com/health /intimacy.

Oppenheimer, Alex. "Homemade Paintballs." Gone Outdoors. Accessed July 14, 2022. goneoutdoors.com/homemade-paintballs-5896472 .html.

Pace, Rachael. "What Is Intellectual Intimacy & Tips to Improve It." Marriage.com. Last modified April 26, 2022. marriage.com/advice /intimacy/what-is-intellectual-intimacy-and-does-it-actually-exist.

Richter, Wolf. "After 17 Years of Falling Ticket Sales, Movie Theaters Got Annihilated in 2020." Wolf Street. January 10, 2021. wolfstreet .com/2021/01/10/movie-theater-ticket-sales-after-falling-for-years -got-annihilated-in-2020.

Shpancer, Noam. "What's in a Kiss?" *Psychology Today.* November 3, 2013. psychologytoday.com/us/blog/insight-therapy/201311 /what-s-in-kiss.

Suttie, Jill. "How Music Bonds Us Together." *Greater Good Magazine.* June 28, 2016. greatergood.berkeley.edu/article/item/how_music _bonds_us_together.

US Department of Agriculture (USDA). "Don't Feed Wildlife." USDA Animal and Plant Health Inspection Service. Last modified July 8, 2022. aphis.usda.gov/aphis/ourfocus/wildlifedamage /dontfeedwildlife/dont-feed-wildlife.

Walsh, Colleen. "What the Nose Knows." *The Harvard Gazette.* February 27, 2020. news.harvard.edu/gazette/story/2020/02 /how-scent-emotion-and-memory-are-intertwined-and-exploited.

Whiten, Samantha Rodman. "When Kissing Stops in a Long Term Relationship." *Dr. Psych Mom* (blog). December 10, 2021. drpsychmom .com/2021/12/10/when-kissing-stops-in-a-long-term-relationship.

Winder, Austin. "Why Knowing Your Partner's Love Language Can Strengthen Your Bond." *Heartmanity's Blog.* Accessed June 8, 2022. blog.heartmanity.com/why-knowing-your-partners-love -language-can-strengthen-your-bond#:~:text=Knowing%20your %20partner's%20love%20language%20allows%20you%20to %20meet%20their,your%20relationship%20on%20deeper% 20levels.

Index

ACKNOWLEDGMENTS

I would like to thank: the Most High for choosing me to give life to this book; Nana, for EVERYTHING; Granddaddy; Kobi; Mom, for recognizing my gifts; Daddy, for your steady belief in me; Grandma; my beautiful sisters: Brigette, Erica, and Gabrielle, love you hard; Aunt Carol, Jack, and Chris; Antonio, for your generous heart; my incredible nieces and nephews; George; Arelis; my amazing tribe of friends; Celeste and Peter for your friendship and legal counsel; Callisto Media; and the singles and couples that allow me to be of service.

ABOUT THE AUTHOR

 **Angela Nicole Holton,** named by Yahoo! as one of their top 10 relationship coaches, is an international dating and relationship coach, speaker, author, and the founder of Love Sanctuary. She is the creator of the Conscious Love and Dating Method Coaching Program, a modern and revolutionary approach toward dating, and the author of *The Secret Method to Conscious Love*. She holds a BA in psychology from the University of California at Berkeley and a master of social work from New York University.

Printed in the USA
CPSIA information can be obtained
at www.ICGtesting.com
LVHW050745171223
766457LV00005B/45